To Galatians,

Thank you for all your

Cinemographic help now

and Into the future

(Kiffer)

PUSH DOWN
AND TURN

PUSH DOWN AND TURN

UNDER AND ABOVE THE INFLUENCE

KIFFER COLE, M.D.

Library of Congress Control Number: 2016907420
ISBN: Hardcover   978-1-5144-9162-1
                   Softcover   978-1-5144-9161-4
                   eBook   978-1-5144-9160-7

Print information available on the last page.

Rev. date: 05/04/2016

To order additional copies of this book, contact:
Xlibris
1-888-795-4274
www.Xlibris.com
Orders@Xlibris.com
727777

To the reader,

I'm writing you the book I wanted to read.

I'm telling you the story I would like to have read at a time in my life when I needed some honesty. I'm telling you the things about my life that I wish someone would have told me about their life, and maybe I wouldn't have felt so very alone. For as long as I can remember, I have felt like I didn't fit in, like there was something wrong with me, that something dark set me apart from the rest of the world. I felt broken and like some integral part of what makes us all human didn't quite work right in me.

As it turns out, that's not true. As it turns out, I just didn't know how to tell other people how screwed up I felt most of the time. I didn't feel safe. And by not feeling safe to express how vulnerable I felt in a very scary world, I decided to create a false self, being confident, arrogant, and invulnerable, while at the same time anesthetizing my real self with drugs. It worked out pretty well, until it didn't. And my life fell apart in a massive way.

I lived most of my life believing everyone else but me had it all together, like they had some secret formula for happiness I wasn't ever told about. I can't tell you what evidence I had for this assertion. I can just tell you that I believed that if people knew me, really knew me, they would hate me as much as I already hated me, and that was a lot.

None of that is true now, and it wasn't true back then.

I found out that when I started revealing the hidden parts of me, the world became less scary. How I came to that realization is the primary reason for this book.

My life fell apart around me one day. Don't get me wrong. I knew it would. It wasn't a surprise. I had been on a fast track headed for destruction for years. A pattern of behaviors that began even in childhood set me up for massive success and destruction.

I want to start by telling you what happened, how it all fell apart, and how a picture-perfect life could crumble in moments and fall through my fingers like ash. Then I want to tell you my story.

I want you to sit down on the porch with me. I've pulled out a shoebox full of the pictures of my life, and I'd like to show them to you, maybe tell you a little story about each one. We may skip around a bit, but I bet if we look through the whole box and you listen real close, you'll start to hear your story too. And that's why we're here after all, to see ourselves in others. The only way I've learned to love me is to love you, warts and all.

Want to see my warts?

Enjoy.

PROLOGUE

"Dr. Cole?"

Her voice seemed to be muddled like she said it through a paper towel tube.

"Did you hear what I said, Dr. Cole?"

I could hear what she was saying, but everything was happening too fast. I was beginning to feel a slight sense of nausea, sitting at my desk staring down at two sheets of paper that said Subpoena across the top. When the two agents had shown up at my office, they sat down, slid these two pieces of paper across my desk, and started talking. I read the words quickly and stopped reading when my eyes lost focus from the fear that was welling from deep inside me.

"Dr. Cole, we need to see the records on these patients, please."

Her voice still seemed distant as my mind raced to find the right words to answer her request. I knew I had a lie for this situation. What was it? The air in my lungs was trapped from the swelling in my throat. I was paralyzed with dread. The room, my office, and my world were closing in around me. It was as if the walls were literally moving, inching closer and closer toward me. I could feel the room shrinking. The ceiling felt as if it was descending toward my head and would, in moments, crush me under the weight.

Say something, I thought. *Say something, goddamit. Say anything!*

I couldn't. My nausea was growing into inevitability.

The two agents shifted uncomfortably from my silence. They waited for a response from me. Confused, I momentarily flashed back to the night before. Memories began flashing into my consciousness.

I was standing in my garage now, reaching into the depths of my golf bag, where I concealed a bottle of Southern Comfort. Retrieving the bottle, I unscrewed the top and took a long pull. The hot liquid hit my mouth and mixed with the pills that were already on my tongue: four methadones. It was the last of my supply for that evening. As I swallowed the pills, nausea hit me in the gut, and I panicked. I couldn't throw up. No. It was the last of my supply, and if I didn't keep them down, I was sure to go into withdrawal and not sleep a wink. I had to keep them down at all costs. Despite my efforts, vomit began to rise from my stomach. I ran to the corner of the house. If I was going to throw up, I could not do it in the garage. As I quickly ran through the open garage and around the corner of the house, bile and liquor were already spewing through my defiantly clenched teeth. I relented and allowed the full regurgitation to occur.

The remnants of my dinner, alcohol, and methadone tablets were emptied onto the grass at my feet. "Fuck," I seethed under my breath after I was able to speak. I looked down at the chunks of undigested material in the yard and could clearly see all four of the methadone tablets. After only the slightest second of hesitation, I reached down and retrieved the slimy pills and held them in my hand. As I looked down at the pills, I could sense there were tears in my eyes. I was unsure if they were from having just vomited or if they were the last vestiges of self-respect leaving my body. I threw the moist pills back in my mouth, and instead of swallowing them, I began to chew. I let the chalky material coat the inside of my mouth and prayed I would not throw up again.

"Dr. Cole, I know this is hard for you, but you really need to talk to us."

Agent Graves's voice led me back from my memory. She and her partner were still seated across my desk. I was still nauseated and realized that it was this feeling that had triggered the memory of last night. I looked down, and the subpoenas were still on my desk.

"We really need to see the records on those patients. Our investigation of you reveals a large number of overlapping narcotics prescriptions being given to these patients, and we need an explanation for this." She paused slightly, choosing her words carefully, and continued, "Based on the pharmacy record we have reviewed, it's clear that no one patient could possibly take the amount of narcotics you are prescribing them."

Oh yes, they can! I wanted to scream. *I do it every day.*

I again retreated into the memories of the months and years leading up to this event. I saw myself sitting in my truck outside countless pharmacies. I kept a prescription pad in my glove compartment, and after taking out the pad, I would choose one of the fictional names I used to obtain pills and write that "person" a supply of narcotics. Late in my addiction, I would also go as far as having preprinted patient labels with completely false information typed on them and use these labels to ensure plausibility. I could leave no room for a pharmacist to doubt that the prescription was authentic in any way, and the labels offered that plausibility. After making sure that the prescription was flawless in every way, I carried the prescription into the pharmacy to get it filled. With a practiced calm demeanor, I presented the prescription at the counter. "Would you like to wait on this, sir?" the pharmacy tech always asked. "Yes," I always answered. I would wait as long as it took.

I chose a seat that offered me the best view of the pharmacist and telepathically guided his actions. From my peripheral vision, over the top of a magazine, I watched. I waited until he held my prescription in his hand. I recognized the shape, the color, and the patient labels on "my" prescription. I silently prayed that he would seamlessly, effortlessly, recognize the obvious validity of the prescription and fill it. I knew I was home free when the pharmacist began fishing for his keys.

In retail pharmacies, narcotics are always kept in a locked location. So when the pharmacist began searching for his keys, I knew he was about to fill the prescription. The sound of those keys got me higher and more excited than the pills ever did. It meant that he was not going to question the prescription. He was not going to question me. He was not going to call the doctor, but more importantly, he was not going to call the police. The sound of a pharmacist's keys metallically clanking and pinging together was the most beautiful sound in the world to me.

I blinked and refocused my attention on Agent Graves.

"Can you produce these patient records for us, Dr. Cole?"

What I said next was shocking.

I said something that was completely foreign and confusing to me. I told her the truth.

"No," I said weakly.

I swallowed hard and continued, "No, I can't." She seemed to breathe a sigh of relief as her shoulders dropped slightly, as if some form of disaster had just been averted, and she relaxed just a little bit.

I forced myself to continue to speak, but seeing her demeanor soften made it easier to continue. "Those patients don't exist," my voice was tremulous, "so their records don't exist. I made them up. I made them all up," I paused and continued, "to get pills for myself."

And with that last comment, my fear, my dread, and my shame rose to a crescendo. I could hold back no longer, and I couldn't resist. With practiced precision, I reached for the garbage can under my desk and vomited. I threw up right in front of these agents.

Years of lies, manipulation, shame, and guilt poured out of my body into that trash can.

And when I was done, when the last bit of sickness had exited from the depths of my soul, I sat back and asked myself out loud, "How did I get here?"

The two agents, wide-eyed and speechless, could only sit in shocked immobility at what they had just witnessed as I asked myself again, "How the hell *did* I get here?"

I

GROWING UP (SORT OF)

Suicide Is Painless

From my vantage point lying on the couch in the living room of my grandparents' house, I could see my grandfather Cunningham dozing next to me in his favorite black leather recliner.

The Benadryl and Demerol my grandmother had given to me through the IV line in my arm was wearing off. I was nine years old.

I vaguely remember being told by my mother earlier that day that I was sick and being carried to my grandparents' house for them to care for me.

As I awoke from the drug-induced haze, I could smell the familiar menthol of my grandfather's Marlboro. I dozed in and out of sleep, but I could still make out the outline of him in his black recliner. With his feet propped on the matching leather ottoman, he too drifted in and out of consciousness. The Marlboro, burning like unattended incense in his left hand, sat precariously scissored between his fingers as they draped over the armrest of the chair; a long curling ash grew from the butt, and smoke rose undisturbed toward the ceiling.

The carpet beneath him was pockmarked with cigarette burns, as was the arm of the chair he was in. He leaned back into an almost-horizontal position, and like the ash at the end of the cigarette, he appeared as though at any moment he would topple over. But he didn't, and it didn't. Instead, both he and his ash remained balanced in perfect alcoholic suspended animation.

Now, to be fair, I never actually saw my grandfather drink. Despite him being constantly, consistently blindingly inebriated, I never saw him put a glass or bottle to his lips. If our family had a mantra, it would be "If you didn't see it, it didn't happen."

We kept secrets.

As the narcotics in my blood stream began to wear off, I became aware of the television on the far end of the room. The opening credits to *MASH* was playing as I watched my grandfather sleep. I listened to the lyrics:

"That suicide is painless . . ."

I watched his body tremor with the ever-present shake that accompanies chronic alcoholism.

"It brings on many changes . . ."

As he shook and struggled to breathe, he was at his most peaceful teetering on the edge of alcoholic unconsciousness and death. The song played on.

"The game of life is hard to play . . ."

I became aware of not only the television now but also the slight pain in my arm from the IV my grandmother had inserted earlier that afternoon.

"I'm gonna lose it anyway . . ."

My mouth was dry from sleeping hard as a result of the drugs. I blinked, trying to watch the images on the television, but couldn't focus yet. The song continued to play.

"The losing card I'll someday lay . . ."

I closed my eyes again, deciding just to listen to the television and the rattling, rasping breaths from my grandfather.

"So this is all I have to say."

When I awoke again, it was at the sound of my grandmother Eunice coming into the room.

"Cunningham," she called out to my grandfather, who was still asleep in his chair. "Wake up."

He didn't move. She had said the words walking past his chair, heading into the adjoining kitchen. Disappearing and then reappearing moments later, she again nonchalantly called out to him as she passed by him sleeping in his chair.

"Cunningham, you're gonna burn the carpet again. Wake up."

This time she stopped and stared down at him with her hands on her hips. When he again exhibited no signs of regaining consciousness, she turned and retrieved an ashtray from the coffee table. With practiced accuracy, she placed the ashtray under the extended ash of his cigarette at the precise moment it broke off from the burning butt and caught it safely before it fell to the carpet. She then removed the Marlboro from between his fingers and placed it too in the ashtray and set it back down on the table.

Dressed in her white nursing uniform, white linens, nursing cap, and white platform heels, Eunice looked as if she had stepped out of a World War II–era VA hospital. After disposing my grandfather's cigarette, she knelt down beside me and began to examine the arm where she had earlier placed the IV.

"Do you feel better, Kiffer?" she asked as she started to peel medical tape away from my arm.

"Yes, I'm fine," I answered sleepily.

I didn't really have any recollection of ever having felt bad, not really. But it was so commonplace for me to receive heavy medications when I was presumed to feel sick that I guess I had been ill. Maybe?

Intravenous fluids, penicillin shots in the ass, and cough syrups of all flavors and varieties were what I had come to associate with illness. I really didn't mind being sick anymore—or whatever version of "sick" necessitated such treatments in my grandmother's eyes.

She continued removing the tape from my arm and, grasping the bevel of the IV catheter, slowly removed it from my vein. As it slid from under the skin, a small pooling of blood formed in the hollow of my elbow. With bare hands, she used a cotton ball to stop the bleeding and placed another piece of tape over the cotton ball. Grasping my hand, she bent my arm into a flexed position and said, "Hold that there."

I knew what to do. I had done it many times before and knew the drill.

She gathered up the IV tubing and the empty bag that had held the fluids she had infused into my body. Standing up, she left the room—I presume to dispose of the bag and tubing.

I lay there for a while holding my arm as instructed and watched the characters on TV. *MASH* had started, and I watched as the doctors and the nurses of the mobile army surgical hospital handled all sorts of disasters. Helicopters brought wounded soldiers in from the field, and the half-drunk, slightly insane staff of the hospital would put them back together.

As I look back on it now, it was not that *dissimilar* to what was happening here in my grandparents' home. Anything that could happen—any ailment, disease, wound, or trauma—was being cared for by the medical expertise of my grandmother Eunice. In fact, we had our very own MASH unit: medicate anything safely at home.

I suppose the *safely* part of that acronym is up for debate. The summer previous, I had injured my finger trying to catch a tennis ball with bare hands. When I had shown the clearly misshapen and swollen pinky finger to my grandmother, later, her reply had been, "C'mon, Kiffer, it was only a tennis ball, right?"

"Yeah, but it really hurts," I'd replied.

"Well, it's not like it was something hard like a baseball," she had responded. "I'm sure it'll be fine."

She then taped a tongue depressor to the underside of my finger, and I went on playing as usual.

Three weeks later, when we were in the orthopedist's office having the finger rebroken and set, I can remember the orthopedist asking my grandmother, "So, Eunice, how long ago did this happen?" (They had worked together at the hospital and were on a first-name basis.)

"Oh, just a couple of weeks ago," she had said. "But . . . you know kids . . ." She turned from the doctor and looked me squarely in the face. "He didn't tell me about it until today."

She had said this with feigned disapproval and a "you better keep your mouth shut and don't embarrass me in front of this doctor" look in her eyes. I had learned to understand those looks early on in my life. In this case and many others like it, I wasn't afraid of outing my grandmother's negligence and her being angry with me and punishing me later. But rather, I was more afraid of my grandmother losing face in front of this doctor. In that moment, I was embarrassed—not embarrassed *for* her, but embarrassed *with* her.

It was as if, as a dysfunctional family, we stuck together at all costs. There was a genuine sense of us-against-the-world loyalty that trumped everything and everyone. Even when we hurt one another, at least we had each other, and that was more important than anything else. It was more important than honesty, integrity, or even safety at times.

And although I'm sure every family has its share of embarrassments and secrets, it was as if ours were self-perpetuating. One area of dysfunction required even more dysfunction to keep the first hidden. And on and on it would go until the only "truth" to be had was whatever could be harvested safely from a therapist's couch years later.

Then, lying on her couch after my IV fluid–narcotic combo treatment (for what was most likely a head cold), I had no idea that this was some seriously dysfunctional shit. It wasn't until I began talking about things like that that there came a resounding "That's fucked-up" response from those seated around me in group therapy. As a child, it was just what happened. As an adult, looking safely back through the locked doors of a medical detox unit, having almost killed myself with narcotics and booze, it made a little more sense. Me sitting on that detox unit was almost an inevitability given I started my life a heavily medicated child keeping secrets.

But I'm getting ahead of myself. Where was I?

Before my grandmother left for her shift at the hospital that day, she stopped again and knelt beside me on the couch.

"Now just lay there and rest, Kiffer," she said. "You are still very sick."

She instinctively reached up and felt my forehead and leaned in close so only I could hear what she said next.

"If you need anything," she said, cutting her eyes toward my dangerously intoxicated grandfather, "you know how to call the hospital, right?"

"Yes," I answered. I knew how to call and ask the operator to transfer me to where my grandmother could be found.

But what she meant was, "*You* are in charge, Kiffer. Dear god, please call me if my alcoholic husband does anything but lay there in that chair and drool!"

"Please call me if he tries to drive anywhere."

She made this last request with wide eyes and a slight nod up and down with her head.

"I will, Grammy," I promised her.

With this, she smiled. Getting to her feet, she shot one last glance at my grandfather and simply stood staring down at him. Her smile faded into something else entirely. It morphed into a look of pure revulsion and disgust. One that would have been better suited on the face of someone watching a child molester being set free from jail on some frivolous legal technicality.

But there was something else there too. Something deeper. Something I would later grow to appreciate inside my own heart: it was defeat. And not the pity one would feel from witnessing someone else's defeat. No. It was the look of realizing her own. The look of an inward recognition that this is where her life, her marriage, her dreams had come to rest—lifeless and inebriate.

Before she left, she turned and smiled down at me one more time and said, "Kiffer, one day you're going to be a doctor. Did you know that? Promise me you're going to make something of your life. You're going to make me so proud, and everyone is going to love you for it."

With that last comment, she left. Moments later I heard the engine of her car roar to life in the adjoining garage and then fade into silence as she pulled out of the driveway and down the road.

With nothing but the sound of the television remaining, I dozed off to sleep again, but it was short-lived.

I was startled awake by the sudden coughing fit from my grandfather. He lurched forward in his chair, desperately clearing soot-filled phlegm from deep inside his chest. I sat up from the couch almost in unison with him and stared as he convulsed, trying to clear his lungs.

When it finally subsided, he sat slightly slumped and exhausted like a losing prizefighter between rounds, breathing heavily.

He turned toward me, only slightly surprised to see me watching him, and fumbled to light a cigarette. After the first deep draw, he removed the Marlboro from his lips and exhaled. And through resultant cloud of smoke, he said, "Let's go for a ride."

Kiddie Porn

A life that most assuredly began with the infinite possibilities of childhood happiness and success for my grandfather Cunningham ended with quiet, alcoholic haze in a bed of knotted bedsheets filthy with his own vomit and urine.

But when I was nine years old, my grandfather unknowingly gave me the greatest gift a young man can be given: access to pornography. And before you judge me too harshly for such an audacious claim, remember, I am just telling you the truth. When a young boy is first introduced to pornography, it is *the* turning point in his young life. Provided, said pornography is not in the hands of some pedophile offering candy and puppies if you just "get into the van, little boy." Because that's just sick.

The kind of porn I'm talking about is just your run-of-the-mill, American-made, homegrown, tits-and-ass smut, and at the time, my grandfather had a stash of smut that marveled even mine today.

During that year of my life, I spent a great deal of time living with my grandparents. My mother was in and out of drug rehab facilities, and depending on her level of mental instability, I would sometimes live with them for weekends or months at a time.

My grandparents lived separately under the same roof. My grandmother had a bedroom on the main floor, and my grandfather had moved into the finished basement/apartment to drink himself to death in private. My memories of my grandfather Cunningham were actually all good or disturbingly bazaar. Despite his eventually lethal alcoholism, he seemed like a pretty decent guy from the standpoint of a nine-year-old. He was a retired military officer who had drunk himself into early retirement and spent all his days during this period of my life blindingly drunk.

I can remember being fascinated going through his personal belongings when he was unconscious and looking at all the medals he had acquired during his military service. I can recall thinking he must have been a very important man to have been given such honors and respecting him for serving in the military. I would later find out that he had entered the military as a result of a plea bargain to avoid going to jail for embezzlement from the company he had worked for in his civilian life. I guess they don't give medals for that.

As a nine-year-old, I can remember my grandfather spending most of his time unconscious. When he was upstairs and away from his basement lair, he would sit in a large black recliner, nodding off and burning cigarette holes in the arms of the chair and in the carpet underneath. Cunningham was an unusually tall man, standing (when he was standing) six feet five inches tall. He was an ominous figure with jet-black hair combed straight back from his face. His nose was red and bulbous from years of alcohol abuse, and I can always remember he smelled funny. I know now that it was just vodka seeping out through his pores combined with the smell of liver failure and cigarette smoke. But at the time, all I knew was that he didn't smell like other people in my life.

When he was still a marginally functional alcoholic, he would take me for car rides to go to the convenience store with him. He would say, "C'mon, Kiffer. Let's go get an ICEE."

So Cunningham and I would set off in his big brown Buick, which looked like it had survived (and dominated) countless fender benders (because it had.)

The Little Giant convenience store was only two miles from the house and was located next to the liquor store. As it turns out, that's what really made it "convenient," but traversing that small distance was always a harrowing experience. My grandfather had a unique way of stopping the Buick at red lights: he would run into the car in front of him!

This was not an occasional occurrence. It happened almost every time we took the small road trip together. We would slow to an almost stop, and wham, God help whoever was in front of us. Sometimes the person we hit would get out of his car to yell at my grandfather and, seeing his state of intoxication, would simply return to their car shaking their head, deciding to forget the incident than deal with a drunk over a slight collision.

When we would arrive at the Little Giant, he would say, "OK, you go get an ICEE, and I'll be right there." We would part ways, and he would rejoin me minutes later with a brown bag, and he would pay for the ICEE. In addition to paying for the ICEE, he would also purchase a magazine. I can remember initially never paying attention to the magazines he would buy, but eventually I began to notice the titles: *Penthouse*, *Playboy*, and the holy grail of them all, *Hustler*. The clerk would put his magazine in a brown paper bag, and we would return to the Buick. I would be carrying my ICEE, and he would be double fisting brown paper bags with liquor and porn. Mission accomplished!

This outing would be repeated several times throughout my nine-year-old, memory and Cunningham would amass a porn collection that most people would consider disturbing but I would find absolutely fascinating.

My grandfather also taught me how to play pool. Cunningham's downstairs apartment was connected to a larger finished room containing a bar and a pool table. The bar had long since fallen into disrepair since my grandfather's drinking had graduated past the need for such extraneous things like mixers, ice, or glasses. He drank straight from the bottle at this point. The pool table, however, was functional, and as long as my grandfather could stay in that state as well, he would teach the art of billiards. Even drunk, he could still play pool, which fascinated me since he wasn't nearly as successful at driving. Using one eye and swaying dangerously, he could still bank shots and place English on a cue ball that made it appear to defy physics.

When he was simply too inebriated to stand any longer, he would return to his bed to finish slipping into unconsciousness and leave me alone to play by myself.

Once when my grandfather was away playing golf at the military base (don't ask me how he accomplished this), I was busying myself doing what would later become a favorite hobby: going through other people's shit. I could busy myself for hours going through his and, later, other people's belongings. It's amazing what other people probably don't want you to find.

(I guess you're probably not going to invite me to house-sit for you now, huh?)

On one such fact-finding mission, I found Cunningham's stash of porn. Piled under his bed were every magazine I had ever personally seen him purchase and many more. Hundreds of magazines thrown carelessly (drunkenly) under his king-size bed. Albeit the bed was low to the ground (since real alcoholics never slept any higher than a height from which they could safely fall), the piles of magazines still almost touched the box springs.

I quickly began thumbing through the porn. With each new page, I felt I was being given secrets and underground information that had been hidden from me for nine years. I was consumed. *My god*, I can remember thinking, *why have they been hiding this from me?* This was quickly followed by, *What the hell is he doing to her? Why is there a midget holding a torch in the corner?* (I had found the *Hustler* by then.) I must have looked through dozens of magazines, enthralled by the glossy pages. They even felt slick to me under my fingers. The paper was even heavy, unlike the wispy pages of my grandmother's discarded issues of *People* magazine.

During my first introduction to porn mags, I even figured out the hierarchy of mainstream straight porn. *Playboy* had just chicks, and they would be wearing less and less clothing with each turn of the page. *Penthouse* actually had guys in the pictorials, but they were only for contrast and were never naked. And then there was *Hustler*, whose images depicted the collision of male and female genitalia in alluringly grotesque detail. I loved it immediately!

My head snapped up from the pages of the *Hustler* at the sound of my grandfather beginning to descend the steps into the basement. I threw the magazines back under the bed and panicked for a moment. He would see me if I ran out the door at this point, so I ducked into his bathroom and eased the door almost shut and turned off the light. I was now successfully trapped. Through the crack in the door, I could see him cross the room and prayed he did not need to use the bathroom. He didn't. He crossed the small crack in the door and climbed onto his bed and turned on the television.

I was breathing hard with fear and stood stone silent, looking out of the small opening between the door and doorframe. I could feel my heart hammering in my chest. His bed was out of sight, but I could clearly see the television. I watched and tried to calm my breathing as he browsed through the channels with the remote until he settled on a channel and the picture came into view. It was then that he unknowingly introduced me to an equally fascinating gift. Apparently, *Playboy* not only made magazines—they also had a television channel!

Images the likes of which I had never seen played out before me in real time. Images just like the ones I had seen statically being portrayed on heavy glossy paper were now alive with illuminated electric sex. It was without a doubt the most pivotal point in my young life. I could not tear my eyes away from the naked gyrations of femininity that were being acted out before me on that screen.

I stood there motionless for a long time, mesmerized by the images. Women in various states of nudity were performing for the camera accompanied by a soundtrack of thumping hard rock riff that seemed to meld perfectly with their movements. The softness of their bodies combined with fluid, sensual movements was inextricably changing me somehow, advancing me, moving me somehow more toward manhood with each successive scene.

I was startled back from my hypnotic state by the sound of my grandfather snoring. My grandfather's advanced alcoholism had transformed him into a near narcoleptic. The fact that he could fall asleep anywhere (especially while driving) was common. I could always tell the depth of his unconsciousness by the volume of his snoring, and now he was deeply asleep. I thought this was my chance. I had to escape my hiding place, and now was the time. I needed to make it out of the bathroom and out of his room.

I lowered my body close to the floor and eased the door open wide enough for me to slide through the crack. I eased my body close to the floor and began to belly-crawl out of the bathroom. Being careful to monitor his snoring to ensure he was still safely asleep, I made my way across the carpeted floor. I passed by the side of his bed and saw the stacks of magazines underneath. I halted my slow progress and reasoned, *Surely he wouldn't miss just one of these magazines.* I could take just one. I angled my direction slightly and wedged myself under the bed and reached with one hand to retrieve one of the magazines. His snoring halted with a choke and a gasp for air. I froze. He was awake.

I lay motionless under the bed, hoping my breathing would be drowned out by the sounds from the television. As I lay flat, breathing in dirt and fibers from the carpet, I could hear him fumbling with the drawer of his bedside table. I felt his weight above me as he rolled back flat onto the bed and was again motionless, or so I thought.

I turned my head and peered from under the bed toward my eventual destination of the door that led out of his bedroom and waited. I was sure I would soon hear his snoring and be clear to make a crawling dash for the door when he was again asleep. Instead, the mattress above my head began to move. The box spring lowered and rose above my head in a rhythmic motion, squeaking with every descent. Up and down . . . up and down. *What is he doing?* I thought. The motion was similar to a small child jumping on the bed above me. Up and down . . . up and down . . .

Then he began to moan!

A low guttural moan was escaping from my grandfather and combined seamlessly with the motion of the bed. The frequency of his thrusting and moaning increased in intensity until it ended abruptly in the crescendo of his self-pleasure until he was again still. And just as quickly as it had begun, it was done. He was soon snoring again.

At this point, I had no idea what I would later in life understand—that my grandfather had been jacking off on the bed above me. I didn't really know at this point what would have been worse: seeing him do it or having him do it literally inches from my head. Either way, I had seen/felt too much for only one day of a nine-year-old's life.

After I was sure he was again soundly asleep, I made my way out of his bedroom with the magazine (I had worked too hard to leave it behind after all). That one day of visual sexual overload may have just sent me into an early and abnormal puberty. I believe it kick-started a flood of testosterone from what had been previously undeveloped testicles and rendered me incapable of ever looking at women the same way from that day forward. I was instantly and irreversibly a sexual creature mesmerized and infatuated with the opposite sex. Half the blood flow that had once gone to my brain would henceforth be shunted to my genitalia, rendering me incapable of making wise decisions when it came to women ever again.

I am eternally grateful to my grandfather, in the most emotionally immature way possible, for all he had shown me that day, whether he was aware of it or not. I am sure Hallmark never made a Thank You card for just such an occasion, but if they had, I'm sure it would go something like this:

> Grandfathers get kinder and wiser as time passes.
> You offered me glimpses of huge tits and asses.
>
> No fishing trips or dating tips could ever really be
> As thoughtful as the gift of pornography.
>
> No grandfather is perfect, but you really helped me see
> How wonderfully perverted life can truly be.
>
> Thank you, Grandpa.
> Kiffer

(If someone from Hallmark is reading this, call my publisher if you want some more material.)

Grandmother of Pearl

After learning everything I needed to know about sex from my alcoholic grandfather, I learned everything I wanted to know about love from my pathologically codependent grandmother, Eunice. What could only be described as a series of disastrously embarrassing encounters with the opposite sex through the years began for me at the age of 9, when I fell hopelessly in love with Amy Allison, the most beautiful girl in third grade.

My grandmother worked the three-to-eleven night shift at the hospital. She always wore a starched white nursing uniform and nursing cap. She wore her cap perched precariously not on her head necessarily but pinned high atop heavily teased gray hair. What kept that hat in place were not Cartery pins or gravity but the overzealous application of Aqua Net after it was already in place, thus cementing it to survive an eight-hour shift at the hospital. It looked as if it would tumble at any instant off the back of her head but never did. Her appearance was remarkable being that I now know her job entailed some of the most repulsive tasks a hospital had to offer. Although I never had the chance to see her at work, I can now imagine her hoisting sweaty, obese patients from beds to wheelchairs, being careful not to yank out urine and rectal tubes in the process. I can imagine her cleaning wounds, holding vomit basins, and performing enemas while never once disrupting the position of that cap or soiling her pristine white uniform. I watched her return home from countless shifts looking just as professional and immaculate as she had when she left for work.

After every shift, Eunice would descend into the basement to check on my grandfather and take his vital signs as he slept in a drunken stupor. She was checking to make sure her husband was neither dead nor in the throes of delirium tremens from alcohol withdrawal. This was a task she performed nightly in the later stages of his life. It was as if he was the final patient she would round on at the end of every night.

She would also return with pockets loaded down with various drugs left over from her shift. At that time, drugs in the hospital were not accounted for the way they are today, and walking out with narcotics was a rather easy task. She would empty her pockets of blister pill packets and vials of intravenous drugs and haphazardly toss them into old shoe boxes and drawers in her bedroom. Years of this practice had netted quite a stash of various medications, most of which were narcotics and controlled substances.

I almost never went to the doctor for illnesses. Instead, it was rather common for me to receive shots of penicillin in her bathroom and even intravenous bags of fluid as I laid on the living room couch watching television. Staying home "sick" from school was an altogether different experience for me compared to other children my age. Eunice was the doctor, nurse, and pharmacist for the family. I reveled even as a child going through her room while she was at work and looking at all the drugs and researching them in the PDR (Physicians' Desk Reference), which she had also stolen from the hospital.

My grandmother didn't only steal from the hospital nor did she only steal pharmaceuticals. Eunice was likely to steal just about anything. At restaurants, she would take things like steak knives, salt and pepper shakers, and she especially liked small ceramic and metal condiment bowels. All these articles would, at some point during the meal, disappear from the table to be stowed away in her ever-present brown leather Aigner handbag. At home, her kitchen became the resting place for hundreds of unmatched utensils and service ware. It was truly an amazing collection. She would also wrap uneaten food in cloth napkins and shove them, grease stains and all, into her bag. This she did even when asking for a to-go box would have been easier. She would often explain this behavior by saying, "People with class do not ask for to-go boxes, Kiffer." And when she said the words *to-go*, she would even lower her voice and hiss the words out between pinched lips with utter disdain like the words stank as they were exiting her mouth.

If I was ever accompanying her to department stores as a child, she would ask me to "hold" things during our shopping adventures, only to inadvertently have me walk out of the store with her booty. Many times we would make it home with costume jewelry, wallets, and gloves she didn't pay for. She most likely did this for plausible deniability lest we get caught and she needed an alibi. I can only imagine what her response would have been should a security guard at Neiman Marcus catch us exiting the store with our bounty, "Well, no, sir, I had no idea he picked this up while we were shopping" and turning to me "Now, Kiffer, you know better than to take things without paying for them. Now give those earrings back to the nice man and tell him you're sorry!"

And although this never happened, I can tell you with assuredness I would have known from experience and the tone of the lie in her voice that I was not to say, "But you told me to hold it." No, I would have said nothing but "Sorry, sir" and handed the jewelry back to the security guard. If there was anything that came as a birthright to me as a member of my family, it was how to telepathically detect when a lie was to be told, when a truth was to be hidden, or when feigned misunderstanding was the best course of action. Growing up in a very unhealthy, alcoholic, codependant home gives even a nine-year-old this mind-reading power. The majority of the "communication" that went on in our home was unspoken!

And so it was only fitting that my alcoholic-enabling, kleptomaniac grandmother, who routinely practiced medicine without a license in her home, was the first person in my life to give me advice on love!

In third grade, I fell in love for the first time with a girl named Amy Allison. I should also note, however, that during this time, I also fell in love with Barbara Mandrell the first time I saw her on television and heard her sing. That should tell you a little something about the maturity of my romantic capacities during this time of my life.

But Amy was real in my life. She sat at a desk across the aisle from me in Mrs. Entricken's third-grade class. Mrs. Entricken was an obese black woman who, according to third-grade lore, was the third-grade teacher you do not want to have. She never smiled and could read the minds of children and, I swear, knew before you knew that you were going to do something to piss her off. She always called me by my last name and would yell out routinely from across the room "Cole! Why aren't you doing your work?" or "Cole, keep your hands to yourself. Don't nobody want you touching them!" Bottom line, the woman was scary and greatly feared. She would often lumber up and down the aisles clairvoyantly scrutinizing and judging the room full of frightened third-graders. At this time, you could still whip students, and it was well-known she kept a paddle in her top desk drawer that resembled an oversized ping-pong paddle with large holes drilled through the surface to reduce wind resistance as it would arc through the air before making contact with third-grade asses.

Despite Mrs. Entricken's totalitarian classroom regime, I would constantly sneak glances at Amy throughout the day. I was unable, once squarely infatuated with her, to think about anything else but her. She had blond hair pulled back into a ponytail that would delicately brush her neck and shoulders when she turned her head. Her eyes were blue and made the air seize in my lungs when I would catch them looking at me. I would oftentimes try to mentally will her to look at me just so I could experience that light-in-the-head feeling I would get when our eyes met.

In the realm of my nine-year-old life, my feelings for Amy were as confusing as they were mysterious. I had absolutely no idea what to do with them. Up until that point, feelings were married to solutions. When I was hungry, I ate. When I was tired, I slept. And when I was bored, I did, well, anything little boys do—get dirty, build things, or break things. Life had been pretty simple up to this point.

Now, I was lost. I could do nothing but stare at this little blonde girl and wonder why the hell I was staring at her. I needed answers. I needed help. And for this, I turned to the only adult in my life, my grandmother Eunice.

Despite her kleptomania and pill hoarding (which, at this time, I had no idea was abnormal in the least), my grandmother seemed like a pretty sensible adult. Or she was the only sensible adult I could turn to for advice. My grandfather Cunningham slipped continually in and out of alcoholic consciousness, and I presumed could offer no insight as to why my mind was being held captive by a little girl in my classroom. But my grandmother, after all, was a girl herself. Surely she would have some answers for me. I decided to ask her.

One night, after a shift at the hospital, I found her unloading pocketfuls of narcotics into the top dresser drawer in her bedroom. I stood looking up at her for some time, rallying the courage to ask for answers to questions I didn't know how to ask. When my silence became uncomfortable, she looked away from her drawer and down at me, and I spoke.

"Grammy?"

"What is it, Kiffer?" she asked, looking at me a little concerned.

"What do I do when I," I double-clutched on the last part of the question, "like a girl?"

Silence filled the small bedroom. I had asked the question staring at my feet but could feel her shocked expression on the top of my head without even looking at her. I asked the question sincerely not knowing the answer. Given that my present knowledge of sexuality came from the pornography I had seen on the pages of my grandfather's magazines, I did not know what to expect her to say. If the pornography was any indication of how men showed affection toward women, I was unsure if I would be up the task. But still, I had to have some answers. I had to know what the hell to do next, and I needed my grandmother at that point to tell me what to do.

"Well," she stammered, "is this a little girl in your class?"

I was irritated. I wasn't prepared to *answer* questions about this. I was barely prepared to *ask* questions about this. I answered reluctantly, "Yes, her name is Amy."

"OK . . . um . . ." she said while continuing to rifle through the narcotics in her dresser drawer. This was not a good sign; she was stalling. I was prepared to turn on my heel, walk away, and study some more *Penthouse* forum letters from my grandfather's stash. The guys who wrote those letters might have some inadvertent advice on young love, right?

Before I could walk away, my grandmother reached into the desperation file of her brain and flung out an answer as if it was an epiphany. Behind a slight gasp of internal recognition, she said, "You need to give her something!" She had my attention. "Yes, you need to give her a present. That's what girls like. They like gifts." She seemed pleased but more relieved with her answer and let out a long exhale she had probably been holding since the conversation started.

She began rummaging through the dresser drawer again. Pushing aside pill packets and vials of narcotics, she withdrew a small square velvet box and said, "I have just the thing a little girl would like." With that, she popped open the black box to reveal a set of pearl earrings. They were inexpensive small earrings, but pearls nonetheless. Had I had any fashion sense at this point in my life, I would have actually considered them tasteful and delicate.

(In point of fact, my grandmother had also probably considered them tasteful and delicate in the store she had found them in. And although I don't specifically remember it, she had probably asked me to "hold" them for her as we walked out of whatever store we had shoplifted them from.)

She handed the box over to me, and I studied the earrings with great intent. *So this was the answer*, I thought. I was relieved. I had made some progress in this process. My grandmother had given me the first move in the plan of attack. Although I still didn't know what the end point was supposed to look like (and still don't to this day), at least I knew what to do next. Excited, I took the box and left her standing there. My guess is she was happy to see me leave and even happier she did not have to answer any more of my questions.

The very next day at school, with the jewelry box stowed safely away in my desk, I sat and waited. We had the type of desks where your school supplies were stored in front of you underneath the writing surface, and I had placed the box in the front next to my pencils and erasers. It looked completely out of place amid the rest of the books and papers and actually almost fell out onto the floor several times as I retrieved things from the desk.

I could see Amy out of the corner of my eye. For some reason, knowing that my plan was to try and give her these earrings, I was afraid to make eye contact with her. Scenarios about how I was going to pass this gift on to her played out in my head. Should I just get her attention and hand it off across the aisle? Should I have wrapped it? Maybe I could put it in her desk if she gets up for some reason, only to have her find it when she returned? Surely at that point she would open the box after she sat back down, realize it was me that had given her the jewelry, and smile. She would look over at me, and I would wink, and then we would . . . well, I didn't know what we would do at that point.

All these scenarios spun around in my head and resulted only in me sitting paralyzed throughout the entire day with indecision. I stole glances at the clock and realized I was running out of time. I was panicked. An unknown mysterious force inside me was driving my desire to pass this gift on to her. My grandmother, after all, was certain this was the right course of action, and I simply had to go through with it.

I was struck with an idea!

As the day was finished, I retrieved the box from my desk and walked slowly to the front of the classroom, where students stored their belongings in cubby holes. They contained things like hats, jackets, and lunch boxes. I retrieved my lunch box and stealthily slipped over to Amy's cubby and opened her lunch box. I slipped the earring box in amid the remains of her lunch and closed the lid. It was done! Well . . . sort of. The box was out of my hands and into her (partial) possession. I had successfully passed the gift onto her without even having to muster up the courage to face her. I then went a step further to ensure she knew I was the one that had left the gift. I retrieved her lunch box and carried it back to her desk for her, smiling as I laid it down on her desk and making sure she knew I was the one who had gotten her lunch box for her. I slipped back down in my desk and waited for the bell to ring to excuse us for the day.

As I walked home from school and for the entire night, my mind played out images of what it would look like when Amy found her gift that night. Surely she would find the earrings and be struck with the very same infatuation for me that I was feeling for her. Privately in her room, she would be seated in front of a mirror, put the earrings in, and turn her head left and right to admire them. She would smile, blush, and be stricken with undying love for me. That was what I thought would happen.

That was not what happened.

The next morning, I seated myself next to Amy, and from across the aisle, I could see she was not wearing her earrings. *That's OK*, I thought. She was surely just saving these semiprecious articles of jewelry for a special occasion and didn't want to "waste" their first wearing on a simple third-grade school day. As I had almost mustered the courage to turn and ask her from across the aisle how she like the gift, Mrs. Entricken came lumbering between us, heading toward the front of the classroom. As she reached the front and turned to face us, the room fell silent. I could see she had something in her hand but could not make out what it was from my vantage point. She then raised her arm, collected globules of fat swaying methodically from her dangling triceps as a result of the movement. And in her raised hand was my (Amy's) jewelry box! She displayed it for the entire class to see before she began to speak.

"One of you kids left this," she paused, looking around at every face in the class before continuing, "box in Amy Allison's lunch yesterday." The disdainful emphasis she put on the word *box* would have been more appropriately used to say the word *turd* or *booger*.

She began pacing back and forth, continuing to hold the small black velvet box above her head, before she continued, "Amy's mother found it last night and brought it to me this morning."

Horrified, it was then that I realized that all my fantasies about Amy finding the jewelry and falling in love with me were in gross error. There had been no little-girl surprise at finding the out-of-place small box. There had been no small little-girl gasp as she clicked open the box and saw the earrings. Because in my haste yesterday, I failed to realize one small detail: little girls don't clean out their lunch boxes—little girls' mothers do!

I sat frozen to my seat with fear as Mrs. Entricken paced like a Brahma bull in front of the class, still holding the box above her head the same way the Statue of Liberty holds her torch. She spoke again, "I want to know who put it there!"

No one spoke. My mind was bloated with panic and pre-embarrassment. It screamed, "Say nothing . . . she doesn't know!" I waited as she continued to speak.

"And I want to know *now*!"

With that last angry question, I could see out of the corner of my eye something move. To my left I could see Mathew Lopez, another student in the class, begin to raise his hand slowly, carefully, and with great fear.

I was stunned. Why was he raising his hand? Was he going to take the rap for this? Why would he do that?

"Yes, Mathew?" Mrs. Entricken said as she acknowledged him.

Instead of speaking, Mathew began lowering his outstretched arm in my direction and extending his index finger slowly until he was pointing squarely at me and, with a tremulous voice, exclaimed, "I saw Cole with a box like that yesterday."

So there it was. Staring down the extended barrel of Mathew Lopez's stubby finger of accusation, I realized I had been found out. The day that I had been sure would bring me the first burgeoning of young love had brought me this: thick, nauseating chunks of embarrassment.

I turned back to the front and saw Mrs. Entricken walking directly toward me. She stopped and stood over me, her gigantic girth shadowing me from both light and hope. She laid the jewelry box down on my desk gently. Rather than slam it to the surface, she simply placed it down. It was not the angry gesture I had expected. As she released the box and I looked up at her, I saw her face was kind. Her eyes were soft, and the corners of her mouth were actually turned slightly up in a knowing and compassionate smile. Somehow I knew in that moment that she knew how I felt. She intuitively sensed my dread and vulnerability. As it turned out, the small gift had penetrated deep into the heart of a woman and touched her soul, only not the woman I had intended it for.

Without a word and without a pause, she turned and headed back to front of the classroom and said, "Well, let's get on with our work then." And with that, the box was never mentioned again.

I placed the box back in my desk both horrified and relieved, two emotions that would describe the majority of my relationships for years to come. I never spoke of the incident again, with Amy or any other person, for that matter. I soon left Mrs. Entricken's classroom and the school as I set off on a journey living with my mother. I would learn many life lessons, but few compare to that of my grandmother's pearls.

How to Leave a Lesbian

"Well then, just get the fuck out!"

I could hear the words screamed from the open door of the trailer. Crouched and terrified in the backseat of our 1974 brown Dodge Arrow, I peered out of the back hatch window through the dead of night into the open door of the trailer.

Minutes before, my mother, Beverly, had pulled me out of my bed in our two-room trailer and hurriedly stowed me into the backseat of the Arrow. It was only after she retreated back into the house that the screaming resumed.

"Just stay the hell gone."

"This was never what I wanted, Kathy," I heard my mother yell from inside the trailer.

Amid door slamming and obscenities, the trailer seemed to rock on its raised cinder block foundation, actually *moving* as Kathy and my mother fought within its depths.

Black trash bags began flying out of the open front door, over the rail of the small wooden deck, and onto the ground. Loaded down with our sparse belongings, I could see from the protection of the backseat of the car the bags flying out of the trailer one after another and landing on the ground near the car.

"Take every goddamn thing you want, Beverly!" I could hear Kathy scream from inside. "Just fucking stay gone!"

Out came another garbage bag hurled through the night air as if accentuating the obscenities.

My ten-year-old mind began to register what was going on after the haze of sleep left me and the thudding beats of my heart began to subside. We were leaving Kathy.

Breaking up is hard. No matter how well adjusted emotionally the couple is (and that was certainly not the case in this situation), it's still heartbreaking. But when two lesbians break up amid overt drug use and lack of any hint of sober-coping skills, well, it can be downright terrifying!

When a man and a woman break up, I've found it runs a pretty standard course. The man finds every reason in the world that it's the woman's fault. He can then retreat into any form of vaginal replacement therapy, which is readily available. This can include anything from another woman, drugs, alcohol, work, self-pity, or righteous indignation; usually a combination of these will suffice.

The woman, sure that the relationship ended due the *man's* lack of communication skills and an overt inability to understand *her* needs, will usually retreat into remorse and self-loathing. She may slip into a cocoon of self-degradation with a firm resolve that she must be completely unworthy of love. She may even pull out pieces of collected memorabilia of the relationship to torture herself with—pictures, ticket stubs, old receipts, the petrified bud of the first rose he gave her. All these items have been carefully stowed in a shoe box tucked on the shelf of the bedroom closet, and she sobs over the memory produced by each one as she pulls it from the box and clutches it to her chest.

(OK, maybe I have done that last thing.)

But the point being, men and women seem to be evolutionarily hardwired to cope with breakups in an orderly albeit emotionally heart-wrenching fashion.

Alternatively, when two women break up, it must be something that genetically the modern human world is not ready for.

I've always been jealous of women who seem to naturally and effortlessly bond with other people on a deeper, more emotional level than I have seen from the masculine species in general—loving others at the soul level, whether it's with a man or another woman. They love with everything that is inside of them, holding nothing back.

So when two women with this galvanizing level of bonding split, it produces the release of emotional energy akin to a nuclear fission reaction. And it's downright scary.

When one woman decides to leave another, it's like when one in a set of Siamese twins decides she is going to leave her sister. Twin A is desperately trying to get away from Twin B, pushing against the connective tissue that has entangled them their whole lives, while Twin B is clutching at her partner and clawing against the searing pain of the separation.

And in the present case of my mother leaving Kathy, it was worse! As I heard them screaming from inside our trailer, I could envision Beverly not only pushing away with all her might against Kathy but then also leaning down with her mouth to gnaw at the stretched and straining human tissue that connected them, taking desperate huge tearing bites, only to look up with a mouthful of ragged skin and blood, pleading, "I am so sorry it had to end like this, Kathy."

(Chomp.)

"You never loved me like I loved you!" Kathy screamed in agony.

(Chomp.)

"I never wanted to hurt you, Kathy!"

(Chomp.)

"But you are hurting me, you lying, deceitful bitch!"

(Chomp.)

And with one last bite, my mother reappeared at the door, running hard for the Arrow, which sat with its engine running in the short gravel driveway.

As I sat in the backseat of our car, I watched my mother gathering the vestiges of our belongings that had been thrown out into the yard. In pair of tight Jordache jeans, halter top, and no shoes, she gathered the bags and threw them into the now-open hatchback of the car. Her blond hair was a mass of tangles; mascara, ruined by tears of anger and fear, ran down her cheeks.

Kathy emerged from the trailer with another armful of loose clothing and flung them into the yard.

She was wearing brown coveralls, her uniform from the maintenance department of the state university where she worked. Of note, it was really the only thing I ever saw her wear. Outside of that and the occasional softball uniform, I was unaware that she owned any other articles of clothing.

She had been wearing them the first time I had ever met her. Six months ago, she had been seated beside my mother on one side of the booth of a Western Sizzlin and me across them. It was then that they had tried to explain to me over our dinner how sometimes women could love each other just like a man and woman loved each other and that we would be moving in with Kathy. And well, that was that. I guess I should be grateful they even took the time to try and explain the situation to me. I don't remember caring much about what they were telling me. After all, my mother had already been married three times by the time I was ten, so I figured Kathy coming on the tail end of three unsuccessful swinging dicks might prove to be a success.

She was not.

Besides her uniform, the only thing I really remember years later was her hairdo. It was short and curly, styled in such a way that looked as if the only missing element was a chin strap.

Six months after my mom and Kathy gave me the eighties' amended version of the birds and the bees talk, they broke up.

As she flung the last of the clothing over the deck rail, she added, "And if you think that sorry excuse for a man is going to make you happy, then you two pieces of shit deserve each other!" With this last statement, I could see her pointing to the front driver's seat of the car.

I turned and realized for the first time that I wasn't alone. Someone else was in the car with me.

Bruce was young, ten years younger that my mother's twenty-nine years, and as if taking a cue from Kathy, he turned and yelled to my mother, "Beverly, just leave the rest of that shit and let's go!"

"Bruce, I need our clothes. I haven't gotten any of Kiffer's things . . ." And she started back in the house.

Bruce opened the car door and grabbed her by the shoulders, halting her progress. He ushered her around and, opening the passenger door, threw her in the car.

Kathy continued screaming from the deck of the trailer, "Kiffer deserves better than you dragging him out in the middle of the night while you chase after some teenager's cock, Beverly!" She began sobbing at this point.

"Fuck you, dike," Bruce said over his shoulder as he slammed the hatchback closed and got back in the car.

Depressing the clutch and putting the Arrow in first, he slammed the gas hard. Gravel sprayed behind us, and hundreds of small stones rattled under the wheel well of the car as it lurched forward; we were gone.

My mother hunched in the passenger seat and sobbed into some loose articles of clothing she still held in her hands.

As Bruce madly shifted gears, accelerating the Arrow past tightly spaced trailers on either side of the road, he said, "Damn, Beverly, why the hell didn't you just come back for that stuff when she was at work?"

"Bruce, I don't know. It's not like I knew she would go insane—"

Wham!

The sound stopped my mother in midsentence, and Bruce slammed the brakes on the car. As we screeched to a halt, Bruce looked over his shoulder back in the direction of our trailer.

"Holy shit, was that a gun?" he asked as he squinted, trying to look past me through the rear window. "Does she have a gun?" he asked as he looked back toward my mother.

"Oh god . . . yes," my mother answered. "You don't think she . . . we have to go back!"

My mother opened her door and started to get out of the car, but Bruce grabbed her, pulling her back hard into her seat.

"You are out of your fucking mind, Beverly! Get back in the car!"

With that, he again threw the car in first, and we were gone again, the acceleration of the Arrow slamming the passenger door shut as we sped off.

As we pulled out of the entrance of Clover Ranch trailer park, police cars' running lights and sirens were pulling in. They paid us no attention as we headed off into the night.

I don't know where the bullet from that gun landed, but much like one fired from the gun of a starter pistol, it heralded the beginning of our new life with Bruce.

On your mark . . .

Get set . . .

Go!

II

ALL GROWN UP: I THINK WE HAVE A PROBLEM HERE

Narcotics Not So Anonymous

As a fourth-year medical student, I started routinely withdrawing from narcotics. This was the first indication in my life that something was seriously wrong with my recreational pill taking. It would later be absolutely confirmed when I found myself picking half-digested pills out of vomit so I could take them again. Waste not, want not! But at this point, the routine withdrawal would scare me into my first Anonymous meeting.

I was living in a rented house near my medical school and doing a rotation at the VA medical center in, of all things, their drug rehab ward. At the time it seemed like such a good idea. The patients were crazy, and I was pretty sure I was crazy, so it seemed like a great fit. I was one of the medical students assigned to work on the inpatient detox ward. I would sit in and sometimes lead groups of patients withdrawing from drugs. The only problem was, so was I! If I wasn't withdrawing, I was high on pills. At this point in my life, those were the only two options: high or miserable.

I supplied myself mainly by stealing drugs from my mother and grandmother when I was home for the weekend, taking enough pills to last me through the week. Invariably, though, I would take all the pills and end up withdrawing on about Thursday, which over time turned into Wednesday, then Tuesday . . . you get the picture. I had no control over my using even early on in my addiction.

Opiate narcotic withdrawals became part of my daily life. It led me to believe that what I had was not so much of a drug problem per se, but a supply problem. I kept running out! I knew from the first time I took drugs that it would be something I would do forever. I ended up being wrong about that, but if you had had been able to probe the depths of my denial-riddled brain, you would have surely seen a galactic-sized hole with a sign that read Place Drugs Here. I believe I was born with that hole, and I had been trying to stick shit in it since I found something that worked.

Drugs worked really well. The first time I took drugs, I didn't get high—I got normal! Every fear and emotional pain I had ever had went away, and it was as if the gates of heaven unlatched and I was escorted in for the first time in my life. If you tell me you have never had that experience with narcotics, then that is precisely why I do not understand you at all. It's also why at this time in my life, whether I was willing to admit it or not, I could not even fathom not taking pills on a regular basis. It had ceased being an option for me. Not having narcotics in my bloodstream, which bathed my brain with relief, was like holding my breath underwater. No matter how hard I could try and stay underwater, I was going to come up for air. I was going to use again, end of discussion.

The insanity of drug addiction was that I would tell myself I was going to quit. And I would believe myself. Every handful of pills I would steal from my mother's medicine bag was "going to be my last!" I would say that countless times throughout my using, and I would believe it countless times. But then the pills would be gone, and I would again sink my head under the water of abstinence . . . and wait. The cravings to use would always come. Like craving for air in a drowning victim, I would panic. Fear of living a life without the drugs that gave me solace and peace was simply too much to bear. I would then succumb to using drugs again, and just like coming up for air, it would be sweet relief.

During my rotation at the VA detoxification ward and drug treatment ward was the first time I became aware of what my life had become. At midweek, I would run out of pills, and the first sign that something was wrong was a general state of unrest, insomnia, and an inability to sit still or be comfortable in any position. My body had an uncontrollable desire to move. The floor under my feet produced pain. The chair under my ass begged me to stand up. The air on my skin was to hot or too cold. Sounds reached into in my brain through my ears like hands and shook it violently. Basically, the world became an intolerable place to be. And the worst part, the truly miserable part, was having to behave as if nothing was wrong. Hell was feeling like this on the inside and having to look like a medical student doing a fourth-year behavioral medicine rotation on the outside.

It was in this state that I helped run groups in the detox center. "Groups" in detox center consist of groups of patients sitting in circles of cafeteria-style chairs (unless you're a dope addict who still has money, then you may get cushion chairs, but if you still have that much money, you're probably not done doing dope) and doing talk therapy. Many issues that would be discussed would be things like how they got into drug treatment, why they used drugs, triggers for using drugs, and other general reasons for unrest (of which there are many in drug treatment).

On one such occasion, my attending physician was called out for another meeting, leaving me alone with a group of twenty middle-aged addicts well into their addiction, with no one to lead them but me. I stared around at faces that had known drug horrors that I would only come to know in my lifetime. Part of me wanted to scream, "Quick, while he's gone, tell me how to avoid this shit! How do I not sit where you're sitting? Please help me!" The other and stronger denial side of me simply began reciting things I had heard other group leaders say, like "So . . . does anyone have anything they need to share?" and "Interesting, and how does that make you feel?" They instantly pegged me for a fraud. One thing addicts can always detect is bullshit. Whether out of learned survival or a general fuck-you attitude, addicts can always flesh out the fakers. If someone is full of shit, they can smell it.

What I didn't forget during the month I spent misguiding this group of addicts were their faces. It was a general recognition of pain and spiritual disharmony that always showed in the eyes. It was deep longing behind the eyes that no amount of alcohol, sex, pills, or therapy could fill. I spent an entire month just watching and listening. I heard the stories and related. I felt the pain and identified. And I witnessed the desperation that I would one day share with each and every one of them.

As was the case with most days, I would return home after a day of endless group therapy to an empty house alone. I had to spend countless hours with nothing to listen to but the neuroses in my own head. The only thing that separated me from a schizophrenic at this point and all points forward during my using was that the voice in my head was my own.

The voice said the following:

"There's no hope."

"You can't tell anyone what's wrong with you, or they will kick you out of school."

"You'll never make it to be a doctor."

"If you ask for help, people will punish you for being weak."

"Just keep faking it the rest of the week, and you can get some more pills this weekend."

"It'll be all right . . . maybe you should get drunk. That'll help."

That was usually the consensus of the endless conversations I would have with myself. And if I didn't have pills, I would drink. I would consume large volumes of alcohol in an attempt to drink away the symptoms of opiate narcotic withdrawal. This failed miserably.

While in withdrawal, I couldn't sleep, sit still, or get comfortable in any shape, form, or fashion. My legs would feel as if they were humming like electricity through a streetlamp, and the thoughts in my brain would race around my head like cars at a NASCAR event. By adding alcohol, nothing happened. I only succeeded in creating a physical state of extreme restlessness but drunk! I would sit in that house for hours drunk enough to pass out but withdrawing so badly I couldn't. If I did manage to sleep, it was for twenty- to thirty-minute bursts throughout the night, only to be awakened by the alarm the next morning still withdrawing and hungover. Then off I would go to the hospital to sit in on some more group therapy.

I convinced myself after a couple weeks of this daily cycle that I was just depressed. That had to be it after all. I was just taking narcotics and drinking to treat the depression, right? After all, I wasn't sad when I took Percocets and OxyContin. I must have a narcotic deficiency in my brain, and anyone else in my situation would take pills like I did, right? I went so far as to go the local bookstore and purchased a depression self-help book that the jacket promised I could "get happy now!" I spent endless sleepless drunken hours doing the written exercises that promised me a new life. In the end, I knew a whole hell of a lot about depression and concluded I need some more pills.

By the end of my month-long rotation at the VA detox center, when my exhaustive denial-based research and self-treatment of my "depression" failed to produce the desired results, I found my first Narcotics Anonymous meeting. I thought, *I take narcotics. I want to be anonymous. Sounds like the right place for me.* I found the number in the phone book and found the meeting location. It was near my house, and I decided to attend that night, anonymously, of course.

I drove to the meeting location and realized that I had passed this house on many occasions driving to and from the hospital. It was a run-down home that looked exactly like the rest of the houses on that street. The only thing that had made it stand out had been the large numbers of black men and women rambling in and out and hanging out on the porch. I could even remember thinking on all those occasions, *Must be a crack house.* And that was the only thought I had given it.

Now I pulled into the parking lot / yard and turned off the ignition. I sat for a long time in the car and debated what I was about to do. *What if it really is a crack house and I got the address wrong? What if they take me hostage? I wonder what it's like to do crack.* I shook the craziness out of my head, opened the door, and walked toward the meeting. On the porch, I was careful not to make eye contact. Staring instead at my footfalls and using my peripheral vision to scan for crack pipes (like I would have known what that looked like), I made my way into house. I found my way to a folding metal chair (the unofficial seat of all Anonymous meetings) and spent the rest of the moments before the meeting inspecting lint on the aged carpet with great intensity. *Don't look up,* I thought. *If you look up, they will talk to you, and you don't know what to say. Just stay long enough to hear how to stop taking pills. I wonder if they know where to get some pills? Don't look up . . .*

Someone spoke, and the meeting started. "Let's have an NA meeting."

Everyone in the meeting shouted in response, "Let's have one!"

My head shot up as a reflex and immediately began to process the room that surrounded me. I was the only white guy in a sea of black men and women. I had suspected this when I was walking in, but now it was real.

Growing up, I had been only one of three white people in an all-black high school. The principal at the time was named Dr. Dinkens and had stopped me in the hall one day and, with a huge smile on his face, had asked me, "So, Kiffer, how does it feel to be the minority for once?" I didn't really know then, but I sure as hell knew now it feels scary as shit!

Faces began turning to notice me (I wasn't exactly blending in at this point), and my fear turned to sheer nausea-inducing horror. Although most of the faces turning to look at me were unfamiliar, some were not! Scattered about the room were people I recognized. They were the faces of some of the men who had been inpatients at the VA detox ward from the previous month's rotation. They were the faces of those people I had stared at day in and day out for an entire month. They were faces of those men who had known me as "Kiffer Cole, medical student." They were the faces of those men who had sat hopeless and empty in front of me day in and day out in the group therapy I had led! I wanted to run. I had never known panic until that very moment, and my heart tried to race out the door before me.

The meeting chairperson in front continued, "Do we have and newcomers who would like us to get to know you better?" A few smatterings of hands popped up around the room. Mine did not. They felt like they had been dipped in wet-cement cinder blocks and been allowed to dry. But so did my entire body at this point. I was paralyzed. *Anonymous my ass,* I thought.

As the men from the VA began to recognize me, they leaned in closer to one another and whispered back and forth and waving at me.

The chairperson continued, "I've asked a friend to read *How It Works* for us," which was followed by a series of readings from well-worn, laminated pieces of paper. Instead of listening, I spent a great deal of time avoiding eye contact with my previous patients, staring intently on things like walls, water heaters, and ceiling tiles and thinking *Oh god . . . oh god . . . oh god . . . just let this get over with.* Of all the horrible scenarios that had passed through my mind about attending that meeting, this situation had never occurred to me. The thought of my patients being at this meeting and recognizing me was devastating. I had envisioned maybe some ritualistic hazing of me as the newcomer, with people cornering me in a room, asking all sorts of questions, and generally embarrassing me. But this, this situation had been out of the realm of possibilities. I began to look around the room for an escape route, but I was trapped. The room had filled after I sat down, and people were actually standing and blocking the exit at this point. I was there to stay.

I envisioned these men returning to the inpatient ward the next day and telling everyone, including my attending physician from the med school, that they had seen me. This would be followed by an intervention by the med school, drug tests, and my eventual dismissal. I played out this scenario in sickening detail. I knew beyond a shadow of a doubt that this was the end of my medical career entirely. *Why the hell had I come here?* I asked myself over and over again. I was nauseated and choked back the vomit that had risen to the back of my throat.

After the readings, people began sharing out loud how life without drugs was so much better. What seemed like endless numbers of people talked about how they were not doing drugs and how much better there life was now. Then an older member of the group said something that seriously pissed me off. He ended his sharing by saying, "And to the newcomer, just remember, you never have to drink or use drugs again!" I was furious. I thought, *I never have to use drugs again, huh? That's the secret? That's all there is to this thing?* I wanted to leap from the chair and say, "I never have to take pills again? From this point forward, I can just stop? Don't you know what happens to me when I don't take pills? I lay awake all night for days at a time. I throw up. I have diarrhea. I shit myself just a little bit every time I cough or sneeze. I have to listen to my own thoughts that tell me over and over again that I do, in fact, have to use . . . Fuck you!"

I didn't say this. I just sat there, and even sitting was becoming difficult to do. I was still in full withdrawal. My legs were screaming at me to move, to get up and walk, to do anything but stay in that seat. But I stayed until the meeting came to an all-too-welcomed close. Everyone at the end stood in a circle, joined arms, and recited the Lord's Prayer. After the *amen*, I didn't leave immediately. One thing I had done while sitting there the entire hour was to formulate a plan. I needed to do some quick damage control.

I let those men who had recognized me come over and talk to me. I had guessed that they would do this judging from their excitement at having recognized me in the first place when I had walked in. And as I suspected, three guys from my addiction group came over and hugged me.

"Hey, man, its god to see you," one of them said.

And another followed by saying, "Yeah, we didn't know you were an addict. Welcome to the group."

I sat my plan into motion and, with false surprise, said, "Oh, no. I'm not an addict. This was just part of my medical school training. They want us to come and sit in on outside meetings and learn . . . No, I'm not an addict."

They looked shocked at my response. But the good thing was, they were buying it! I was a pretty good liar even at this point in my addiction. I could be so convincing that I could make people believe my bullshit enough they would go and tell someone else the same story, convinced the bullshit was true. So I waited for their response, being careful not to say too much and seem too anxious that they believe me.

They looked at me for a moment and simply said in return, "Well, this meeting is a closed meeting for addicts only. They do have open meetings where outside people can come if they want."

I responded quickly, "Oh, well, I should come to those meetings instead. Sorry, guys." I shook hands with them, turned on my heels, and exited the room quickly. As I made my way out to the car, I wondered how successful I had been. I even formulated a lie to tell the medical school if any of those men did decide to tell anyone I had been there. I reasoned I could tell them that my rotation in the detox ward had been so interesting to me that I had decided to do some outside research and attend a Narcotics Anonymous meeting. I would even add that yes, I had seen a few of our patients there, but I couldn't say who. It was supposed to be, after all, anonymous!

Content with my plan for diversion should the need arise, I got back in my car to return home and drink myself into semisleep since I was out of pills. After that meeting, I wouldn't set foot in another nor draw a sober breath for seven more years.

Cheers!

Catfight

On many nights, my wife would make the mistake of going to work and leaving me at home alone and, thus, in very dangerous company. Her not being there worked out very well for me because without human accountability, I could drink and take pills exactly the way I wanted to.

This was, of course, without interruption. Human interaction can be an irritating variable in the life of an addict and alcoholic, especially if that human is sober. This is because they are a constant source of what I was continually trying to escape: reality.

I was a third-year medical resident and she a nurse at the same hospital in Atlanta. We lived in a small apartment south of town, and our schedules often conflicted, leaving me at home alone often. I never planned it that way, but it left me home alone many nights in various stages of alcoholic disrepair.

My favorite hobby during this period of my life was to take pills. MS Contin, an oral form of morphine, made life just tolerable enough on a daily basis. It made basic human tasks—like being a doctor, conversing with others, and breathing—comfortable for me. I didn't drink daily, but when I did, I never drank like other people, normal people. Whereas some people drink socially, sipping on watered-down glasses of whatever, I preferred whiskey. It had to be straight and warm. I always marveled at how other people drink "socially," enhancing the experience of being around friends and enjoying their company and eventually leaving some drink half-finished because they were feeling just a little tipsy. My drinking was like jumping out of an airplane without a parachute on purposefully. It was fun at first but was going to end quickly and disastrously in the end. When I broke the seal on a bottle, it was just like stepping out of that plane, and it was always bad.

On one night in particular, I was at home alone and had been chewing morphine pills and watching television. I was almost through a fifth of whiskey when our cat, Mavis, jumped onto the couch next to me. I had bought Mavis for my wife, Ann, for her birthday when we were first married. I got her at a pet rescue center at a local pet superstore. She was a kitten when I got her, and I remember deciding out of all the kittens in the various cages, she had appealed to me most because she was hunkered behind the rest of the kittens in the cage and not playing with any of them. She was curled behind the mass of raucous cats, not interacting in the least. It was as if she was saying, "I'm not taking part in any of these games. I'm not putting on a show for these humans. They can just kiss my ass." Her to-hell-with-all-this attitude appealed to me, and I purchased her on the spot. As it turns out, however, what I thought was aloofness toward life turned out later to be only the first signs feline psychosis and that she was probably just plotting ways in which to kill the other kittens in the cage by scratching their eyes out and watching them bleed to death from the empty sockets, all while licking clean her blood-soaked claws. I would have to learn this the hard way.

As she sat on the couch next to me, I fumbled to grab her and hold her cradled in my arms. I sat bleary-eyed and drunkenly rubbed her stomach as she purred deceptively, looking back at me and waiting. I reached for another pull off my drink when a blinding pain ripped through my left eye. It happened so quickly it was difficult for me to register exactly what had happened. The pain felt like someone shooting acid into my brain though a needle inserted directly into my pupil. It wasn't until I looked down to see Mavis recoiling her claws and heard her growling that I realized this cat who had just been purring happily had attacked me. In one swift motion, Mavis had mounted a feline-ninja sneak attack and had tried to blind me.

I let out a guttural scream and stood up so quickly Mavis flew out of my lap and was launched across the living room into the television broadside and hit the screen with a thud.

OK . . . I threw her into the television.

I reached up with my hand and felt the sticky blood that had almost instantly began pouring from my eye and ran/stumbled into the bathroom to survey the damage. After clicking on the light, I quickly registered that my eyeball itself was undamaged. But beneath the lower lid was a laceration that was steadily streaming blood. Also squeezing grotesquely through the ragged incision were small bits of fat and tissue, in which I carefully used my finger to push back into the hole. I held pressure on the wound for a few moments with a washcloth to stop the bleeding and checked again to make sure my eyeball was still intact. I stood back from the mirror and was instantly more sober than I had been moments before.

I quickly recounted what the hell had just happened and began, for the first time in my life, to experience homicidal ideations . . . toward my cat.

I screamed out loud "Mavis!" and surprised even myself with the rage that was beginning to billow forth out of me. As the pain continued to drive through my skull, I backed away from the mirror and turned to leave the bathroom to hunt down the perpetrator of this heinous cat-on-human hate crime I had just been a victim of.

I marched back into the living room to find my assailant with only one thought in mind, *Tomorrow, I will have to go and buy my wife a new cat.*

I found her cowering behind the couch. I flung the couch forward, rolling it upside-down across the room, and screamed, "You fucking cat!" My rage surprised even me, and sensing the impending danger, Mavis turned, stood her ground, lowered her head, and hunched her back. As I stood over her, she hissed and growled while looking me directly in the eyes. Her paw shot out in my direction with lightening speed over and over, swiping through the air with claws fully extended. I was incensed. This cat did not even have the decency to run from me. She was standing her ground, challenging me to take retaliation for her attack. She was taunting me!

I reached down to grab her by the neck just as she arched a claw-laden paw through the air and deeply sliced open a wound on the back of my hand. I recoiled back and clutched my hand to my chest, pausing only long enough to inspect the newest wound delivered by our family pet, and slurred/hissed under my breath, "Oh, you are dead now."

Sensing I was not going to be able to match Mavis in hand-to-paw combat, I turned and made my way back into the bathroom. Flinging open the closet, I retrieved one of my wife's new Ralph Lauren bath towels then marched into the kitchen and found the roll of wide electrical tape under the sink. I began to prepare. I rolled the towel thickly around my hand and forearm and secured it in place with wide loops of grey tape. The towel-tape covered and protected my upper extremity well, but given the ferocity of my opponent, it would have to be tested. Finding a fondue fork in a drawer, I stabbed healthily at my new cloth armor to ensure its durability. Satisfied the fork had been unable to find my flesh underneath the towel, I set out once again to track down Mavis.

Sweating and breathing heavily by this point, I found her. She was waiting for me in the hallway, again maintaining her attack posture. With ears back and head again low to the floor, she began growling again. Cat growls, I realized, are much different than dog growls. They are more ominous and menacing, rising and lowering in octave with almost a human quality. As she began again to slash at the air between us with her claws, I began to feel something unexpected: fear! It occured to me at this point that this very small mammal had somehow managed to nearly blind me, ward off an attack, and now had me afraid of her. Fear quickly turned to half-drunk fury, and I reached down with my towel-laden arm to grab her and shake all nine lives out of this animal!

But I had made an error in calculating my attack. In covering my arm with the towel, I was unable to effectively grab the cat and succeeded only in thickly punching her as if wearing a boxing glove. She took the weak, ineffective blow with ease and pounced on my arm, sinking the claws of all four paws into the towel. I pulled my arm back, only to find she was attached now.

I jumped up and violently tried to shake her off my arm. Running back down the hall, I literally could not fling the madly hissing and growling cat off the towel that I had earlier securely taped to my arm. I fell back hard against the hallway wall and used the nearby doorframe for leverage to peel Mavis from my arm, wedging the wood molding between her and the towel, being careful not to use my unprotected arm at all for fear of her biting or scratching the exposed flesh. She jumped off and ran for cover elsewhere in the apartment.

I slid down the doorframe and breathed heavily. I could feel now that my eye was bleeding again and wiped at the wound with the towel and looked at the blood for confirmation. Returning to the bathroom mirror, I could see the wound at this point would definitely need repair. I quickly assessed my situation. I was in no condition to be behind the wheel of a car to drive myself anywhere to have the wound sutured, and there was absolutely no way in hell I was calling an ambulance. Whiskey mentality took over, and the solution to this problem became clear. *I'm a doctor*, I thought. *I sew lacerations all the time. How hard could it be to sew myself up?* It was the kind of thinking that you would have to be drunk to understand.

Exiting the bathroom, I removed the towel and tape from my arm and quickly located my medical bag and retrieved the items I would need for the job: suture, needle driver, scissors, anesthetic, syringe, and another glass of whiskey. I arranged the items on the bathroom counter and set to work. After pulling up enough anesthetic in the syringe, I approached my lower eyelid with the needle to inject the lidocaine and almost punctured the globe of my eye immediately! Apparently, when performing these procedures on other human beings in the hospital, I had been undrunk all those countless times with steadier hands. I would have to recalculate my timing based on drunk time. So I leaned forward over the counter, steadied my hands on the mirror, and *slowly* injected the interior of the wound in preparation for the repair.

When I was satisfied that the wound beneath my eye was numb, I prepared to place the first suture. I quickly realized that the major problem would be reversing all the movements of suturing, taking into account I was operating on my reflection in the mirror. Every practiced maneuver would need to be the mirror image of what I had been accustomed to performing. Left would appear right, and vice versa, in the mirror. This slight aberrance was easily overcome, and I set to work. Approaching the lower half of the wound with the curved needle, I grabbed the flesh with the needle and thread the nylon through the skin. I then used the needle to grab the upper wound edge, the one closest to the eyeball itself, and immediately, my vision went double! I screamed "Shit!" I had put the needle into the eyeball itself and forced my left eye downward while my right eye remained in place—instant double vision.

Horrified, I removed the needle and realized I would again have to reverse the entire process, starting first with the upper wound edge and then the lower, thus pointing the needle away from my eye for the rest of the procedure. Drink and learn!

The rest of the sutures went in flawlessly, three in all, and the wound was closed. I left all the bloody and used instruments in the sink and set out to find Mavis.

I rationalized that facing my cat as I had been trying to do would be fruitless, and I had to come up with a better plan. I found the broom to use as a tool to simply and not so gently usher the cat out of the apartment. Having been an indoor cat, my hope was that loose in the neighborhood, she may be found by someone else and taken in as their own, maybe some family ignorant of her sadistic and psychotic tendencies. Or better yet, maybe one of the Vietnamese families in the apartment complex may decide to have her over for "dinner." Either way, the cat would have to go!

I didn't care so much at this point to kill or simply maim the cat. I simply wanted it gone. I didn't have the emotional or physical fortitude to do battle anymore, so my plan at this point was to simply herd Mavis outside with the broom. I opened the patio door and, with broom in hand, turned to find the feline, only to find out she had found me. Crouched and again growling, she stood her ground firmly in front of me. Amid the disarray of the living room, with the couch upturned and pillows strewn about the floor, I stood face-to-face with her again.

I jabbed at her with the end of the broom, and she shifted only slightly, swiping madly at the bristle with her claws. I slid to the left, hoping to flank her and force her through the now-open door. My foot landed awkwardly on the pillow, and I lost my balance. Falling to the floor, my full weight thudded onto the carpet. Instead of fleeing out the open door, Mavis retreated back down the hall and into the bathroom.

My anger rose again, but not at the cat this time but at myself. Even my severely inebriated brain registered the ridiculousness of the situation. Rising, I decided to gather my senses and set about to replace the couch and cushions in their correct place. Wielding my broom, I returned to the bathroom to find the cat hunkered down between the small space between the wall and the toilet. I crouched and thrust the broom repeatedly at her. She let out a series of hissing and guttural moaning but held her position despite being pelted by the bristles of the broom.

Next, to my horror and disgust, she began urinating! Streams of acrid cat pee poured and sprayed from her bladder, filling the small bathroom with a putrid odor. The liquid ran onto the floor, and aerosolized liquid coated the Sheetrock wall next to the toilet. Nausea and hatred rose to the surface of my senses as I tried to use the broom to try and pry the cat from behind the toilet. One final effort succeeded in wrenching her from her position, and she leaped past me.

I ran madly behind her, leaving the stench of the bathroom, only to catch a slight glimpse of her tail and haunches rounding the corner of the patio door and into the dead of night. She was gone! I quickly closed the door and bathed in my success, only briefly.

I sat on the couch and tried to wrap my brain around what had just transpired. With a mixture of whiskey and morphine bathing the synapses of my brain, I sat. I recounted the events. I reasoned and rationalized. Had anyone heard this catastrophe? I thought. Had someone called the police, and would I soon be explaining this debacle to uniformed officers at my door? I needed plausible deniability! I had to clean up the apartment so the conversation with the officers would go something like this: "Why, no, officers, I have no idea what you are talking about . . . A fight? Well, no, there is no one home but me. Someone must be mistaken."

It was then that the odor permeating the apartment from the bathroom again became apparent to me. I would have to clean up the evidence/pee!

I set about filling a small bucket with warm water and soap, retrieved a sponge from beneath the kitchen sink, and set out for the bathroom. I knelt down next to the toilet to survey the damage and immediately recoiled. Stuck to the wall, amid the moist stains of feline fluid, were small brown flecks of shit! It was cat diarrhea. In her terror, Mavis not only pissed on the wall but defecated as well. I had literally scared the shit out of her.

The revelation of what lay before me was simply too much for my wet mind to handle or intellectualize. I dropped the sponge back into the bucket. I lay down fully now on the floor, resting my head on the mat in front of the toilet, and slipped into a mire of self-pity. I was exhausted. My morphine high was all but ruined, save the dull and distant thudding in my brain thanks to the alcohol. What had happened? I didn't deserve this. Self-loathing and shame slipped into the pit of my stomach, and I curled into a fetal position and faded into unconsciousness. I passed out.

I was startled to awareness by a scream, "What the hell happened here?"

It was the next morning, and the sound of Ann's voice vaulted me into consciousness. I sat up and blearily began to focus on the face of my wife standing over me in the doorway of the bathroom.

"What are you doing on the floor?"

My mind began to process. What was I doing on the floor? My brain sputtered into pitiful action and tried to register . . . well, anything. I was on the floor. This was true. Why?

"What is that smell?" she asked, holding her mouth over her nose.

As I slowly let my vision adjust to the lights in the room, the memory of the night before came back to me in a macabre montage of images. For an alcoholic, regaining consciousness is nothing at all like waking up from a restful night's sleep. I quickly struggled to pull my battle-laden, hungover body up from the floor, steadying myself on the toilet and then the counter. I prepared for the invariable dizziness that accompanied such a feat. It was truly a practiced skill for any real alcoholic and an absolute necessity lest I go crashing back to the floor. I now stood before my wife, swaying slightly, with a bucket of now-cold water at my feet and the aroma of kitty piss and excrement heavy in the air.

"What happened to your eye?"

We stood face-to-face for what felt like minutes, but I'm sure it was only seconds. I imagine if my life had had a soundtrack at this moment, it would surely have been playing the *Final Jeopardy* jingle. It would have certainly have been the only appropriate song in this scene from my life. I then said the only thing that seemed reasonable to say in response.

"Cat fight."

Magical Vaginal Mystery Tour

My headache woke up before I did, and my arm was asleep. At some point during the early morning hours, it had fallen off the side of my grandmother's couch while I slept and was now basically a phantom limb. I fumbled wildly for my watch, which I had set to go off only three hours previously and was now chirping for attention. Using my functional hand, I silenced the watch.

I then checked to ensure that the fentanyl patches I had placed on the skin of my shoulder were still in place. My pill-taking habit had reached such proportions that using a transdermal approach to getting drugs into my body had seemed much more reasonable. The patches stuck to the skin like tape and delivered narcotics to the wearer steadily over a seventy-two-hour period, thus negating the need to continually chew up and swallow pills. The result was, I was high *all* the time. To state it better, I was not withdrawing all the time. I lay there for a moment trying to recall the events of the night previous and decided it would be a fruitless effort.

After my shift in the ER the day before, which, as a medical resident, I had many, it had seemed like a reasonable idea to detour from my route home and have a few drinks at one of my favorite bars in my old hometown in the suburbs. My wife was out of town, and I did not have to report back to the ER until the next morning. One drink turned into . . . well, a lot, and I decided to sleep on my grandmother's couch instead of risking a long drive back across town.

I rose to my feet and quickly realized my vision was not right. Everything was blurry despite blinking several times to try and correct the effects a hangover can have on eyesight. I staggered into bathroom and quickly realized I was missing one contact lens. Along with parts of my memory, I had apparently lost the contact lens as well. Looking into the mirror, I closed one eye and then the next to determine which eye was functional and then weighed my options. I could look for the contact lens in the couch and decided I did not have time for that. I could remove the remaining contact and endure my severely impaired vision and hope I would not have to suture any wounds that day. Or I could leave the remaining contact in place and use my good eye to perform any necessary procedures. This was the option I took.

Glancing/squinting at my watch, I realized I would not have time for a shower. I stuck my head under the bathroom sink and combed flat my hair. I slipped back into the scrubs I had worn the day before and headed into town for my shift in the ER.

"Good morning, sunshine," said my attending as I stepped through the trauma bay doors and back into the ER, which felt like I had just left. "Long night?" he added as I walked past him sitting at the nurses' station. I responded only with a grunt. I knew I must have looked as bad as I felt and was not ready to explain anything.

The attending physician in a training hospital is the head physician. Residents worked under the tutelage of these physicians during their training and answered to them before delivering any medical care. My attending on this day was known for being particularly sadistic and hard on the residents. His name was Dr. V. He, of course, had a longer name, and it was difficult to pronounce, so he was known only as V throughout the hospital. He was a short white man with gray and thinning hair who chain-smoked outside the ER when it was not so busy. Since the hospital was an urban trauma center, it was busy all the time, so Dr. V stayed in a constant state of nicotine withdrawal. And it showed.

"We've been waiting on you," he said, raising a chart for me to see. "I've got a good case for you." This, of course, meant he had a difficult or disgusting case for me that he in no way wanted to handle himself. He slid the chart across the raised work station toward me and only smiled. I picked up the chart and said, "Thanks."

In the emergency room, patients waited on gurneys behind curtains, which gave the ER a darkly comedic *Let's Make a Deal* feel. I stood outside the curtain and, closing one eye, read the patient's chief complaint. It read Possible GI Bleed. *Well, that's not so bad*, I thought. *Maybe Dr. V is going a little soft.* That was until I stepped behind the curtain to lay eyes on my first patient.

It was an enormous black woman who, although lying comfortably on the gurney, was literally falling off both sides of the bed. Her girth was such that the rails on the gurney could not have been lifted to secure her in place. Her fat enveloped and draped over the sides, and had I not known the gurney existed, I would have sworn she was suspended in midair.

I at once understood Dr. V's zeal in handing me the chart as I had walked through the door. Given her chief complaint of potential GI bleed, he knew what I would figure out immediately. She was going to need a rectal exam!

"You the doctor?" she asked.

I nodded in response. "Yes, ma'am. I am Dr. Cole."

"Good. I been shittin' out blood all night. Y'all got to help me." She shifted slightly as she said this, and her weight made the metallic structure of the gurney squeak in protest.

"Yes, ma'am, I will help, but first I need to get a stool sample to test it for blood." I swallowed hard and continued, "Could you roll over so I can do a rectal exam?"

Her eyes widened with surprise as she saw me begin placing a latex glove on my hand and understood I was serious. She began to comply by heaving her weight from side to side to gain momentum for the maneuver. She rolled, scooted, grunted, and pulled her girth for what seemed like an eternity to leverage her weight onto her left side. I was certain the woman would go crashing onto the floor, ending up as a meat suit covering several fractured bones. But alas, she did not. After several minutes of struggle, she succeeded in ending up in the position I had requested. I laid out a stool specimen card on which I would smear a sample of her stool after I had retrieved it from her rectum. I then liberally applied K-Y Jelly to my fingers and turned my attention back to my patient.

There was a problem. Where was her ass? Before me was a mass of thick fatty skinfolds traversing the expanse of her lower back to the backs of her thighs. I was briefly paralyzed with indecision. Which fold was the right fold? Having clear vision in only one eye certainly did not help matters, but I honestly could not tell. In the end, I decided on a crevice that would most likely be hiding her anus. With a well-lubricated gloved hand, I thrust my fingers deep into the folds.

She screamed immediately, "Lordy, son . . . you in my hoohoo!"

Time froze. Just for a moment, the only movement I was aware of was the reverberating sound waves of the word *hoohoo*. Her explicative was sure to be heard by anyone with ears outside the thin curtain separating us from the rest of the ER. She had said the word very loud.

Realizing what I had done, I removed my fingers from her vagina. The withdrawal resulted in a wet sucking sound that can only be produced by combining latex, lubricating jelly, and female genitalia. Trust me, I'm a doctor! I directed my effort northward, found her rectum, and scooped out enough stool to test for blood, and I was finished.

I exited the room / curtained cubicle with my specimen only to various nurses huddled together laughing and looking over their shoulders at me. My suspicions were correct when assuming that everyone in the ER had heard my patient's explicative upon my inadvertent defilement of her.

"I got another one for you," Dr. V stated with way too much satisfaction for me to feel comfortable. He waved anther chart in the air and grinned and said, "Vaginal discharge."

He handed the chart over and grinned. My head was beginning to hurt from the embarrassment of the previous case, stress, and only having one good eye to look out of. I took the chart from him and thumbed through it on my way to find the patient behind the next curtain. Knowing that a pelvic exam would be required (an intended vaginal exam this time), I grabbed one of the nurses to assist me in the procedure. Still giggling, one of the regular ER nurses agreed to help me, and we slipped behind the next patient's curtain to find her already on the exam table with her legs in stirrups.

The odor was unmistakable. Vaginas have an unparalleled ability to produce some of the most noxious aromas ever produced. There are very few things in this world that can compete for top honors in this department like a good case of crotch rot can. After recognizing the smell, I recognized the patient. She was a young white girl who frequented the ER and still had smatterings of makeup from the night before and, in addition to her other odor, still smelled of stale cigarette smoke and cheap perfume. She was a stripper, and like most strippers, she did not have health insurance. Young women such as herself would frequent the ER for issues such as these, being that they could not afford a regular doctor nor were they very interested in any health maintenance a regular doctor could provide. I actually have a great respect for strippers and their trade. Lord knows I have enjoyed those services many times over in my life (but that's another story, and don't worry, we'll get to it). Also, they were working. Unlike a lot of people who frequented the ER, they actually had jobs. That is not to say that many of the jobless who came into the ER could expect others to pay to see their naked gyrating bodies, but I digress.

"What seems to be the problem?" I asked, sitting down on the stool between her legs.

"There is something wrong with my cat," she answered, and upon lifting the sheet covering her "cat," I was forced to agree. Oozing from the orifice was a thick brown fluid that was obviously responsible for the aroma filling the room. As I placed the latex gloves on my hands, the nurse began handing instruments to me at arm's length, trying to stay as far away she possibly could. I took the speculum and inserted it into the stripper's vagina and immediately diagnosed the problem. Reaching into the cavity before me, I used forceps to grasp and retrieve what looked like a large cotton ball saturated with brown pus and blood.

It's time for a quick stripper sociology lesson.

Strippers work hard. Whether it's to support a family or a raging drug habit, they put in more hours than many members of the nonstripper workforce. Many times they cannot be bothered with taking time off from work during that time of the month. So instead of staying at home and losing money during their menstrual cycle, a simple solution is to insert a tampon and cut the exposed string that is normally attached. Being that in their line of work, displaying a vagina with a string dangling from it may cut down on the tips!

The downside is, it makes removing the tampon a little more difficult and, as was the case with this particular patient, also leads to forgetting one was placed at all. Depending on how long it took to remember the tampon, a raging infection can ensue in the meantime.

After placing the pus-soaked tampon in a specimen container (held at arm's length by my nurse), I directed my attention back to the vagina at hand to reinspect. Upon further investigation, I delivered three more saturated tampons (sans string) and handed them over to my nurse.

After being certain there were no more to be removed, I exited the room in hopes that the nurse may explain to the patient proper vaginal hygiene. I wasn't holding my breath. Or maybe I was, since on the other side of the curtain, I felt the need to take one long deep inhalation of some nonputrid ER air.

I walked toward the nurses' station only to see Dr. V holding out yet another chart.

Residents in the hospital are truly the epitomes of skilled slave labor. They put in long hours, with little pay, doing the worst jobs imaginable. But this was getting a bit ridiculous. I had come into work late, hungover, and smelling like a mixture of body odor and lint from my grandmother's couch. But did I really deserve this much punishment? I was a resident with a massive drug problem. Wasn't that enough?

As I took the chart from his hands, he smiled and said, "Consider this one a gift." I glanced down at the chief complaint, closed one eye, and read Pelvic Pain. That meant only one thing: another vaginal exam! How could that be a gift? I turned to find the correct curtain and again retrieved another unsuspecting female nurse to assist me. Upon entering the cubicle, I understood immediately what Dr. V had meant.

Lying before me in stirrups was a middle-aged woman who was actually very attractive! She was well put together and, despite being in a rather compromising position, looked dignified. This was certainly a rarity in the ER. Her red shoulder-length hair was clean and not matted with vomit or lice. Her designer blouse was clean and looked like something that had been actually stored on a hanger in some closet in a middle-income home. She was actually wearing a bra. And the most surprising of all was the fact that she had a husband with her.

He was standing next to her at the head of the gurney and holding her hand. I felt the need to do something I rarely did. I smiled, introduced myself, and shook both of their hands.

"Hi, I'm Dr. Cole. It's very nice to meet you."

Her husband spoke first, extending his hand. "Thank you for seeing my wife. We appreciate it. We are visiting Atlanta, and she started having some pain," he paused, cut his eyes toward his wife's vagina, which was covered with a sheet, and finished, "down there."

I immediately began to feel like a real doctor. Attractive people who were probably used to going to doctor's offices with aquariums in the foyer, music playing over a very expensive PA, and nonstrippers in the waiting room were asking me for help. Maybe Dr. V had given me a gift after all. I straightened up a little and tried to will my body to stink just a little less. As I sat down on the stool between this beautiful woman's legs, I tried to say the most non–drug-addict, nonhungover doctor thing I can say, "Well, let's take a look, shall we?" I was feeling very important.

I glanced at my nurse and back to the husband, whose head was just visible above the sheet as I raised it over my patient's knees. He was watching my movements intently and, with what I imagine, was great confidence at this point. Her vagina was well-groomed and without even a hint of pus. I even remember smiling at this point.

I asked the nurse for a speculum, which she handed to me with what I sensed was a feeling of pride at working with a doctor of my caliber. I took the speculum and began to insert it into this woman's beautiful, uninfected vagina.

That was when things went horribly wrong!

I am very accustomed to doing medical procedure in a regimented fashion. In addition to the methodical and repetitive ways in which I handle medical instruments, I also say the same things to the patients as I do procedures to keep them apprised of what is coming next. For instance, before giving an injection, I would say, "This will sting a little," and before setting a broken bone, I would say, "We're gonna do this on the count of three, OK?" With respect to vaginal exams, before inserting the speculum, I always say, "You're going to feel a little pressure with this, OK?" I *always* say this.

On this particular occasion, whether as a result of my over-blown ego, the relative beauty of my patient, or the anxiety of her doting husband looking on, what I said this time was:

"You're going to feel a little *pleasure* with this, OK?"

I froze. Speculum in hand, I was paralyzed by embarrassment. Had I really just said that out loud? The instruments my nurse had been holding slipped from her hand and went crashing onto the metal cart beside me. Yep, she'd heard it. I'd said it out loud.

I didn't look up for fear that if I saw the husband's face, actually look him in the eye, the reality of what I had said would just be too real. I did the only thing I knew to do, which was to quickly finish the exam. I stood up and, without pausing, said, "Everything looks normal here. We'll have to order an ultrasound, and we'll know more then." I removed my gloves and exited the room never taking my eyes off the floor.

At this point in my short career as a physician, I had said many stupid things, but this was by far the most embarrassing. I needed a drink! The fentanyl patches stuck to my arm were not doing the trick to erase this bit of reality at all. I guess it could have been worse, but at this point, I really didn't know how.

Then it got worse. Dr. V, seeing me exit the curtained cubicle, approached me with another chart in hand. "Hey, Cole, Wanda Black is here!"

My heart sank. My face still red with embarrassment, I took the chart from his hand. Wanda Black was a frequent flier to our ER. She was a diabetic prostitute and crack addict who regularly presented to our ER in various stages of complete disrepair. Living on the street, smoking crack, and having terrible diabetes forced her into the hospital all the time. And did I mention she only had one eye?

Wanda had lost her eye to a fungal infection years ago as a result of her diabetes. As with many diabetics, she had succumbed to a terrible infection that had necessitated surgeons removing the globe of her eye as well as all the surrounding tissue. This had left her with a gaping hole where her eye should have been. So large was the cavernous socket that she could not even have been fitted for a prosthetic eye, so she wore an eye patch, which gave her the appearance of a pirate. So to summarize, my next patient was a diabetic, crack-smoking prostitute pirate. The hits just kept on coming.

As I lumbered to find what awaited me behind the next curtain, Dr. V called back to me, saying, "Come find me when you get done, Cole . . . I'll keep an eye out for ya!" I could feel him smiling behind me, but there was no way in hell I was going to turn around and give him the pleasure of acknowledging . . . well, a pretty good joke.

Sliding back the curtain, I saw Wanda seated upright on the gurney. She was frail, and wearing her eye patch, I half-expected her to say, "Ahoy, matey!" She, of course, did not.

"What seems to be the problem today, Wanda?" I asked. We were, by this point, on a first-name basis.

"Doc, there's somethin' wrong with my eyehole!" She lifted the eye patch to reveal the horrifying remains of what used to be her eye. Out of sheer will, I grabbed a light off the wall and peered into the depths of her skull to examine what she was talking about. Inside the hole, which could have accommodated a small child's fist, was a lake of pus. Putrid infection emanated from the hole and began to ooze down her cheek when she tilted her head forward. I recoiled and replaced the eye patch over the hole.

"Wanda, we're gonna have to get a sample of this and send it to the lab," I said.

"That other doctor already did that . . . a long time ago," she responded. "Y'all gotta fix me!"

"OK, Wanda." I replaced the light on the wall and turned to leave. Dr. V was seated at the nurses' station, easily identifiable with the shit-eating grin on his face.

"What did you think about that, Cole?" he asked/laughed.

"I think you're an asshole for making me look at that since you already worked it up." You'd have to know that it really was OK for me to call my boss an asshole. When people work together for long periods of time doing what we do, pleasantries like "sir" and "ma'am" quickly get thrown out of our vocabulary.

"I just wanted you to see her. It makes what I'm going to tell you next . . . well, better!"

I didn't understand his evasiveness, but I soon would.

"Well, what did the lab say was growing in her eye?" I asked. He quickly found the lab slip from microbiology and handed it to me. As I read the results, he simultaneously said them out loud, "Gonorrhea!"

My mind was reeling. How in the world did she get gonorrhea in her eye socket? How does a prostitute get a sexually transmitted disease in her . . .

The reality of the answer was just too horrifying for me to handle at this point. It was just too repulsive to be true. As if reading my mind, Dr. V punctuated the depravity by saying, "What some men will pay to do . . . huh?"

I believe in that moment, I came as close as I have ever come to giving up on humanity.

I sat down hard at the desk next to him solemnly, and I silently recounted the day's events: I had defiled a large black woman's vagina, pulled infected tampons out of another, and made a Freudian pass at yet another. I surmised that in a day full of vaginas, Wanda's case seemed to fit right in.

Smile! You're on Candid Camera

My hands gripped the sides of the porcelain sink to steady myself. *Just don't pass out,* I said to myself. *Don't pass out . . . don't pass out . . .* I Just kept repeating these words as I swayed back and forth precariously close to doing just that. I had just taken a large dose of the drug clonidine in an effort to ward off the withdrawal symptoms I was experiencing. Clonidine was a common blood pressure medicine that can ameliorate some of the withdrawal symptoms that come from not having the drugs I was now hopelessly addicted to. I knew it would not get me high but would suffice in keeping the full effects of opiate withdrawal from incapacitating me. The only problem was the side effects of the clonidine: dry mouth, sweating, and severe low blood pressure.

Standing (barely) in the bathroom of my family practice residency outpatient clinic, I struggled to maintain consciousness. I looked up at the mirror in front of me and was horrified at what I saw. A slight sheen of sweat covered the pasty pallor of my face. It dripped down my chin and was being collected by the oxford collar and tie that seemed to be strangling my neck. My pupils were pinpoints, and my lips were chapped despite the moisture of the sweat that was collecting below my nostrils. The side effects of the clonidine were obvious. Although this drug was protecting me from the more obvious signs of opiate withdrawal, it could not hide the fact that I was in very bad shape physically.

I desperately tried to mentally focus myself into being, or at least appearing to be, a functional human being. "Pull it together, fuckhead," I hissed at myself under my breath lest someone outside that bathroom hear me. It was, after all, a flurry of usual activity in a busy clinic. Nurses were bringing patients into rooms, preparing for the afternoon. Attending physicians and other residents were preparing to begin seeing patients. I could hear the familiar hiss of blood pressure cuffs and the accompanying small talk of a busy family practice office . . . and I hated it. I hated it all in that moment.

I was at a stage of my training in which I was allowed to see patients by myself but only under the watchful eye of my attending physicians. Although they did not accompany me into rooms, they would instead be viewing the encounter via a camera mounted in the upper corner of every exam room. Typically, two of the attending physicians would be stationed in a separate and private room. They would be seated in front of a monitor, where they could watch and listen to the encounter between young residents and their patients. The attendings would critique the medical history taking and exam skills of the residents and review the encounter with the young doctors afterward. I had seen and treated many patients under these circumstances before, but on this day, there was one difference: I would be doing it in full opiate withdrawal and suffering the side effects of a powerful blood pressure medicine.

Fear gripped me as I stared at my sickly visage in the small bathroom mirror. How was I going to pull this off? Half my daily life was consumed by getting and using drugs, and the other half had become consumed with finding ways to hide the fact I was hopelessly addicted to those drugs. In my spare time, I was busy trying to get through the rest of my training to become a doctor. I lived in incessant bone-chilling fear that I would be found out and lose everything I had worked so hard to become. I knew beyond a shadow of a doubt that if I was found out or if I dared ask for help with my drug problem, I would simply be kicked out of my residency program and be sent directly to jail. It was with this ever-present anxiety that I finally found the courage to exit that bathroom and try and continue the facade I had so intricately created for myself.

I took a deep breath and stepped out into the hall. I was immediately met with a flurry of activity around me. Nurses hardly noticed me as they were busy with their daily activities. They simply walked around me and carried out their tasks. No one seemed to notice my gingerly gate and the fact that I was steadying myself with one hand on the wall as I walked toward the exam rooms.

"Hello, Dr. Cole," one nurse said as she passed by me, escorting a patient into a room. "I put your first patient in room three. He's a new patient to the office," she said over her shoulder as she passed by.

"Thank you," I said and continued toward the room she had directed me to. My words sounded thick to me as a result of my severely dry mouth, but she did not seem to notice. *I can pull this off,* I thought. *I can make it through this day and find some pills after work. It will all be OK. Just keep it together, Kiffer.*

Before entering the room to see my first patient of the afternoon, I stuck my head into the video monitoring room to ensure my attendings were seated in their usual places in front of the monitors. As I opened the door, the room was dark, but I could see two figures seated in front of TV screens. As they turned to see who had opened the door, my heart seized momentarily. One of the physicians who would be watching me was not only an attending but the residency program director himself, Dr. B! *My god*, I thought, *this day just gets better and better.*

Dr. B was not only my program director but had been my physician as a child. After giving up his private practice, he had started the residency program and held the distinguished position as the director. After I had gotten into medical school, he had taken me under his wing and had assured me that I could have a coveted position in his residency program. Of all the attendings in the program, his approval meant the most to me. Seeing him seated in front of that monitor, I was struck with a deep sense of dread. Would I disappoint him today? Would he find out about my secret? I could not let that happen. I nodded politely at him. "Are you ready?" he asked as he smiled back at me. "Yes, sir," I wasted no time in answering, and I closed the door.

My breathing was far too rapid and shallow as I turned toward room 3 to see the first patient. I blinked to clear my vision. The clonidine was distorting my pupil size, making everything seem blurry and hazy. I stood in front of room 3, my stethoscope draped professionally around my neck, and I took one last slow breath. Shifting into my full actor persona, I took the chart off the rack beside the door. I pulled the corners of my mouth deliberately into a smile and entered the room.

The man seated on the exam table in front of me looked up and smiled stupidly. "Hey, man," he said with a thick southern drawl. "I'm here."

The dread I had felt only moments ago turned to frank panic. Air ceased to move in and out of my lungs, and my stomach felt like it dropped like a brick to the pit of my bowels. I knew this man, and not in a way I would ever like to know any other human being in that moment. I recognized him immediately as someone I had met just the night before.

Memories, thick and viscous, flowed back into my consciousness. Smoke, alcohol, pounding music, and empty promises rose from the shallow but murky occurrences of the night before. They played out again in vivid detail, and I was transported back to a night I now didn't want to remember . . .

"You want another shot of Jack, Doc?" the bartender yelled over the music.

"Yes!" I screamed and nodded approval. I watched her pour a healthy three fingers' worth of warm whiskey into a shot glass and slide it toward me. Without letting the glass come to complete rest on the bar, I took it and drank it. Then after chasing the shot with the beer I held in the other hand, I slid the glass back to her. During this process, which had been repeated at least four times already that night, I hardly noticed the stranger ease up next to me at the bar until he yelled into my ear.

"She called you Doc, man. Are you really a doctor?"

"Yeah," I said without looking at him, trying hard to speak with the whiskey still burning my vocal cords. I turned to see who had asked me this question. The man standing next to me was dressed in khaki shorts and was wearing a pressed oxford shirt unbuttoned below his chest hair and sleeves tightly rolled up to his elbows. He was tan, too tan to have come from anything else but a tanning bed, and he was grinning widely at me. His precancerous bronze skin made his teeth glow like mother of pearl. His receding, bleached hair was styled in a mullet that hung loosely to the nape of his neck. In that moment, I could almost feel the silent protestations of his stylist as he asked her to cut his hair in that fashion and she had reluctantly agreed.

"My name's Rick, man." He extended a hand equipped with a pinky ring and gold bracelet. I shook it and tried to focus my eyes, which were having difficulty seeing through the whiskey and pills that were now coursing through my body. "What kind of doctor are you?" he continued his inquisition.

"I'm a family practice doctor," I answered, leaning close to his ear to be heard over the dance music.

The bar was alive with people moving around us. Loud and low lit, it had all the regular players. Most of the men were dressed similar to Rick, which, for the late nineties bar scene, was the semisleaze mating uniform of choice. The women, fueled by alcohol, estrogen, and crank, scurried around us as well. The air was dense with hairspray, cigarette smoke, and dollar-a-squirt bathroom Polo cologne. The ambience was a thick mixture of ingredients primed for sex and regret (always in that order). Couples gyrated drunkenly on the dance floor for the sole purpose of bringing denim-clad genitalia into close rhythmic proximity, with nothing between them and an unwanted pregnancy but thin fabric. In other words, it was perfect.

Rick lingered next to me at the bar, sipping on a drink and looking uncomfortable after the initiation of our brief conversation. He stole glances my way and looked like he wanted to say something else as he shifted nervously back and forth. *Great*, I thought. *This gay guy is working up the courage to hit on me.* As I contemplated my exit strategy and surveyed the bar for anywhere else to stand and get drunk(er), he spoke again.

"You want a valium, man?"

The question took a moment to register in my mind. I thought I heard him incorrectly through the loud music and must have looked confused. To confirm his question, he began digging in the front pocket of his shorts. He withdrew his hand and produced a small blue pill that, from experience, I knew was indeed valium. I was shocked. I was shocked not by the fact that Rick was carrying a pocketful of pills in his shorts because I myself had mastered the art of carrying pills on me at all times and feeding on them sporadically like M&M's. No, this was not what surprised me. What confused me was why Rick was offering his pills to me. I would have never, and I mean never, offered up a sampling of my own supply to a total stranger.

My shock and disbelief must have certainly registered on my face because Rick quickly closed his hand and returned the pill to his pocket. As if reading my mind, he quickly said, "I'm not gay, man." His too-white smile quickly faded and what remained in his eyes was another emotion: shame. He looked away quickly as if trying to pretend he had not made the offer at all, and I realized what he had already told me. No, he was not gay. He was something else entirely—two things, as a matter of fact. He was just stupid and lonely. I immediately felt sorry for him. There was now an uncomfortable silence that I tried to break.

"That's OK, buddy, don't worry about it," I said.

He smiled and replied, "Yeah, that's OK. You're a doctor anyway. You can probably get all the pills you ever wanted, huh?"

He didn't know how right he really was. Little did he know, my own pill habit had escalated to monstrous proportions. So much so that if I didn't have narcotics in my body at all times, I would enter into horrifying withdrawals. My life had become about having enough pills at all times that withdrawal never occurred. What had become the search to get high many years ago had turned into only the avoidance of withdrawal. I had mastered the dark arts of pill acquisition. His offering of a single valium, which probably seemed significant to him, made me laugh inside. I could swallow handfuls of these pills at a time and actually had just that very night.

He continued, "You think if I came to your office," he paused, working up the courage, "you could prescribe me some valium?"

I let the question linger in the air for a moment amid the smoke and the noise. I took a pull off my beer and began to feel something surge inside me. It was a feeling that was all too familiar to me. It was a feeling that would later in my life become even more dangerous and life-threatening than even the narcotics addiction. It was my ego. It was overblown self-importance. It was false pride. It was vanity.

I sat my beer down on the bar and looked into his eager face. His embarrassment was fading and was being replaced by a longing I recognized. I again felt sorry for him. Pity combined with vanity bubbled up from me and answered before rational thought could.

"Sure," I said with a slight flippant shrug of my shoulders. "Come see me anytime."

Just as the words exited my mouth, I knew it had been a terrible offer to make to this complete stranger. Not even the alcohol I had been consuming could convince my brain that this had been a good idea on any level. I had, after all, only recently been given the title of Dr. Cole." I didn't even see patients at the office without monitored supervision. Yet here I was promising a complete stranger that I would write him a prescription for controlled substances if he would only come see me in the office. I immediately wanted to grab my words, snatch them from midair, and shove them back into my mouth the moment that I spoke them. But it was too late. His lips peeled back into a grin, revealing all those over-bleached teeth. He was elated.

"Where is your office?"

Begrudgingly, I dug into my pocket and produced one of the small business cards that my training program had printed up for all the residents to give out. On it was printed my name, office number, and location of the office. Even as I handed Rick the card, I actually doubted he would ever come see me. I don't know if it was as much doubt as hope that he would not come see me. I had, after all, given my card to dozens of people (mostly women) I wanted to impress, and none of them had actually ever come to the office to see me as patients. I doubted Rick would actually come either. He took the card and studied it intently.

"Damn," he said in disbelief. "You really are a doctor."

I took another pull off my beer and basked in my overblown self-importance. "Just give the office a call," I said. "They will give you an appointment with me."

"I will," said Rick. He shot me one final smile and retreated into the swelling mass of bar people and was gone.

"You want another shot, Doc?" the bartender asked.

I redirected my attention back to the voice that had asked me this laughingly rhetorical question, and I answered, "Absolutely." And with that, Rick was forgotten. He would be only a blip on my narcotic- and alcohol-laden radar screen, but not for long . . .

My consciousness blinked back into reality, back to the present moment. I was again standing in the family practice clinic. It had only taken a fraction of a second to recall the inebriated events of the night before. Seated on the exam table in front of me was Rick!

He was still wearing the clothes he had been in the night before and the same stupid too-white grin. The door to the exam room closed automatically behind me, trapping me in the room with Rick. I stood there face-to-face with him, acutely aware now of what was playing out before me. The man I had promised narcotics to the night before was seated expectantly in front of me. A small camera was mounted over my left shoulder and was recording everything that was about to happen. Simultaneously, in a room down the hall, were two of my superiors about to watch and listen to exactly what was going to be said in this room. This was possibly the most frightening moment of my life.

I had spent years hiding my secret life of drugs and lies from people, especially my superiors. I had always believed that if anyone around me knew about my drug problem, they would discard me (along with my career) like debris scattered along the highway of life. I was now locked in a video-monitored room with another human being who could blow the lid off what I was. I had never before wanted to lose consciousness and simply die any more than I had in that moment. I had to think fast. I had to fix this now.

Rick began to speak, "Hey, Doc—" I could not let him talk. I stopped him abruptly.

PUSH DOWN AND TURN   57

"Hello, Mr.," I paused. I didn't even know his last name. I glanced quickly down at the chart in my hands, "Delatore. I see you are here about your anxiety problem." My mind was racing with fear.

"No," Rick continued, looking a little confused. "I want some valium. Remember—"

I cut him off again, "Well, I need to tell you that narcotics are not the best way to treat anxiety problems . . ." Rick looked even more confused. He was obviously realizing he was not having the same conversation that he had had with me the night before. He opened his mouth to speak again, but I stopped him. "As a matter of fact, we have many other medications to deal with anxiety that are not controlled substances and will do a much better job for you."

I sat down on the stool next to Rick at this point and began pontificating about the many ways anxiety can be treated without the use of narcotics. The longer I spoke, the more confused he looked. Although he tried many times to break into my soliloquy, I would not let him.

My professional presentation to Rick could have been read verbatim from any medical textbook written on the subject of anxiety disorders, and had there ever been given an Oscar for a recorded doctor's visit, I would surely be given that award amid all my adoring fans. Never letting Rick say even a word, I spoke about pharmacologic therapy, cognitive behavioral therapy, lifestyle modifications, and counseling. The longer I spoke, the more glassy-eyed Rick became and totally lost in the things I was saying to him.

At the end of the one-sided dissertation, I had written Rick a prescription for a nonnarcotic medication, made him a referral to a counselor, and shook his hand. Before he could utter so much as a syllable, I escorted him out of the room, down the hall, and straight toward the checkout desk. I left him there looking dumbfounded and speechless.

I'm getting away with this was my only thought as I left Rick behind. *I'm getting away with this again.*

I walked unsteadily back to the video-monitoring room where my superiors were seated, having just watched my interaction take place with Rick. The clonidine was still coursing through my body, but the adrenaline from my fear blunted its effects somewhat. I entered the room, and my attendings turned to see me open the door. I sat down to receive my feedback on the interaction that had just taken place. Behind them, the video-monitoring screen showed only the empty room that I had just exited.

"That was a very good treatment plan, Dr. Cole," Dr. B said. "I like how you addressed all the components of treatment for generalized anxiety disorder."

The other attending spoke, "And you didn't give in to his request for valium either."

Dr. B continued, "Maybe next time," he paused for the right words, "you could let the patient talk a little more and give him the chance to tell you a little more about himself."

I smiled, faking embarrassment about his criticism, and shook my head. "You're right," I replied. "I just got the feeling that he was a drug seeker, and I didn't want to play in to his manipulation." Both attendings smiled with approval and shook their heads in understanding.

"Good job, Dr. Cole," they both said. "Now go see your next patient."

I stood to exit the room and walked back out into the hall. Although my heart still felt like a bass drum inside my chest and I was still unsteady from the clonidine, I knew I had gotten away with it once again. I had successfully evaded disaster. I had yet again lied and manipulated my way out of reality. I had maneuvered my way back into a life of deception and further pain—all in all a pretty successful start to the afternoon.

Head Case

Life as a first-year intern is harsh, especially in the hospital. After four years of medical school, during which every ounce of data that had been gathered about modern Eastern medicine is collectively shoved down the gullet of medical students, the real work begins.

Residency is a time when young doctors begin reaching down into the bowels of *real* medical practice, getting their hands wet (literally) sometimes in the flesh of live patients and making real-time life-and-death decisions. It's not always pretty. For the most part, there is a tremendous amount of oversight from advanced residents or learned older doctors called attending physicians. But many times, young residents, accompanied by their limited knowledge and skills, are all that stand between the life and death of a patient.

My first few months of residency were spent serving on the general surgical service. Waking up at four in the morning to make it to the hospital by five to make rounds on postsurgical patients from the previous day was followed by spending hours on my feet assisting attendings during the actual surgeries themselves.

Every third day was an on-call day, where I would spend the night in the hospital and oversee critically ill surgical patients in the intensive care unit (ICU) and respond to new trauma cases that would be brought to the hospital that would require an extensive amount of intensive management.

My first assisted surgical case was Beverly.

She was a young thirty-five-year-old mother undergoing gastric bypass surgery for obesity. As is usually the case, the first time I met her, she was already under general anesthesia, intubated on a breathing machine called a ventilator, and prepped and waiting in the surgical suite.

I stood for four hours across the attending physician who was performing the complex rerouting of her bowels to limit the amount of food she would be able to consume postoperatively and, thus, lose weight, which effectively meant her body would go into a continuous starvation state and consume itself in order to stay alive.

Assisting meant I would hold gauze sponges, suction blood and debris out of the surgical field, and cut sutures. It also meant I would answer endless questions from the attending regarding the surgery itself, the history of the procedure, and the postoperative care, a justified form of hazing called pimping in the underground medical vernacular, spoken only between those in the medical field. There is a collection of words and phrases only used behind the scenes of the medical iron curtain, which, if ever would reach the ears of the patient or their family, would produce horror and disdain for the medical profession at large.

In Beverly's case, assisting also meant enduring hours of jokes on the part of the attending physician, Dr. Carter, whose bank of jokes was limited to only a single one-liner: "That's what she said last night."

Any and all comments made by the surrounding surgical assist team were potential triggers for Dr. Carter's one-line, one-man stand-up routine:

Anesthesiologist: "Are you almost finished?"
Dr. Carter: "That's what she said last night."
Nurse: "I think that instrument is too large."
Dr. Carter: "That's what she said last night."
Float nurse: "Is that probe sterile?"
Dr. Carter: "That's what she said . . ."

On and on it would go, interrupted only by his occasional pimping question meant on the surface to teach me but effectively only resulted in open ridicule at my lack of experience and knowledge.

After the surgery, which went late into the day, I returned to my call room to sleep, being that I was scheduled to be in the hospital all night.

If I was needed, my ever-present pager would go off and wake me from sleep.

I was scheduled to be on-call with an upper-level surgical resident named Pratt Singer, whom I had only just met a few days prior. I was sure that if I was needed, Pratt would surely hunt me down.

Pratt didn't walk down the hall of the hospital like most of us would walk, easing with comfortable strides and rhythmic arm motions. No, his motions would be considered by most onlookers as dance-like but, at the same time, chaotic. Although his left leg seemed to function normally, the right leg would fly forward in a high step gait that used to remind me of high-stepping horses. It would then flop down to the ground in a lifeless slapping motion. It was almost as if he were wearing an invisible diving fin on that side and had to compensate for the long length of the fin. His upper body, which seemed to not be communicating at all with the lower body, was doing its own thing. His arms slipped out randomly from his torso and without coordination even with each other. They would slither rather than swing as if he were a conductor leading an orchestra in a slow and meaningful piece of music.

All this would have seemed commonplace if Pratt had been a patient on the brain injury ward of the hospital and had been undergoing extensive neurological rehabilitation. But this was not the case. Pratt was the doctor, a fourth-year surgical resident in charge of treating the patients, not the patient himself.

Pratt hadn't been always been this way. The year previous, as a result of a severe motor vehicle collision, he had sustained a severe brain injury that left him with significant neurological trauma and the resulting permanent movement disorder. Just before the accident, he had secured a prestigious neurosurgery fellowship, which, along with any hope of normal movement, had disappeared. The general surgery service kept him on as a resident in training even after the accident out of a sense of loyalty or pity—how much of either, I will never know.

Pratt strode/clopped down the hall and stopped at my call room door in the middle of the night as I laid unconscious on the other side. His knocking woke me from a sound sleep, and I opened the door to see him standing on the other side.

"C'mon, Cole . . . *sllllrrrrrrrpppppppp* . . . wake up."

Did I mention Pratt's mouth didn't work quite right either? On his inhalation between words, he would audibly slurp as if his lips were glued together save one small opening in the corner of his mouth to allow for air to entrain into his lungs. It produced an audible punctuation to the end of everything that he said.

"What are we doing?" I asked sleepily.

"A ventriculostomy . . . *slllrrrrrppppp* . . . c'mon, or the patient's gonna die for sure . . . *slllrrrrrppppp* . . . Got an . . . an intracranial hemorrhage!"

What he had just said began to register with me as he stood unsteadily before me. An intracranial hemorrhage was bleeding inside the brain. And he was right. The patient was going to die, and soon, if we didn't do something. He beckoned for me to c'mon with his hand.

"You go on ahead," I told him. "I'll catch up."

He looked at me quizzically but turned and began walking/shuffling down the hall. The surgical intensive care unit was five floors down, and the way that he walked, I knew I could catch up with him. After all, I had something I needed to do. It was something I always did.

After closing the door, I turned and reached into my bag beside the bed and withdrew an amber-colored bottle filled with hydrocodone cough syrup. Well, it was a half-filled bottle that had been full only four hours before. I pushed down, turned, and removed the cap. Putting the bottle to my lips, I filled the entire cavity of my mouth with the sugary liquid, relaxing and expanding my cheeks to accept as much as my mouth would hold, and swallowed. I had long since abandoned any traditional measuring apparatus for my drug use. Teaspoons had given way to tablespoon, and this had given way to mouthfuls as my only appropriate dose measurement. I knew that mouthful would buy me exactly four hours before the withdrawals would set in. That should give me enough time, and God forbid if it didn't!

I replaced the cap and set off to catch up with Pratt.

The ICU, even at 3:00 a.m., was electric with activity. Fifteen-by-fifteen-foot alcoves, side by side, lined the outer perimeter of the basement floor of Atlanta Medical Center. AMC was a level 2 trauma center that was rivaled only by Grady Memorial Hospital in the acuity of the trauma cases it would see. Being a trauma center in Atlanta meant we would accept severe motor vehicle injuries, gunshot wounds, major fractures, spinal cord injuries, and of course, intracranial hemorrhages. It was the type of facility that smaller hospitals would transfer very sick patients to for treatment.

Each ICU alcove could be separated from the hallway in front by a curtain, but at 3:00 a.m., all the curtains would typically be drawn back, exposing the medical horrors inside. Most of the more intensive care occurred in the middle of the night, when family visiting hours didn't interrupt some of the more inhumane procedures nurses and doctors would have to perform on patients. It was in these hours that wounds would be cleansed of bacteria and dead tissue, surgical drains would be emptied of various ungodly smelling fluids, and comatose patients would be stripped naked and their bodies and various orifices would be cleaned.

All this was necessary. All the tubes and the needles, all the sutures and the machines, all the doctors and the nurses—all were made necessary because of one thing: fear. Our society's growing and ever-present fear and loathing of the concept of death has created an even more terrifying reality: that of modern medicine. You see, anything is justifiable in science and medicine if it extends that most precious commodity called life. And when anything is justifiable, the result is a grotesque amalgamation of torture and self-perpetuating, dogged scientific determination. The only component that appears to be lost at times is that of compassion.

Walking down the hallway to find Pratt was like leisurely walking past cages at the zoo, but instead of each new room revealing some exotic animal, each bay displayed human bodies in various states of horrific physical and emotional disrepair. At this stage of my training, I made a habit of looking in each room and making mental notes about each patient I saw past the open curtain, summarizing in my mind what

I saw there lest I be called to do anything to or for that patient, which, as the first-year intern doctor, was always a possibility. As I walked, I began to feel the hydrocodone take effect. I silently summarized each patient in my head.

Open abdominal wound . . .
(Walking.)
Open pelvic fracture . . .
(Walking.)
Closed head injury . . .
(Walking.)
Gunshot wound to the chest . . .
(Walking.)
Gunshot wound to the . . .everywhere . . .
(Walking.)
Spinal cord injury . . . .I think?
(Walking.)
OMG . . . I have no Idea . . . That guy needs a doctor!

Overwhelmed, I gave up looking into the rooms and made my way toward Pratt, whom I saw at the end of the hallway waiting on me. He nodded at me to come into the patient's room, and he pulled the curtain behind us, artificially cutting us off from the outside bustling of the frenzied surgical ICU. I was startled to see the patient. Lying there was a black man, unconscious, with the head of his bed at a forty-five degree angle. A ventilator tube trailed out of his mouth and was rudely taped to his cheek to keep it from falling out. His eyes, which were open and lifeless, bulged from the sockets and looked like they were going to be jettisoned from his head at any moment. It unconsciously made me want to duck my head away from his face save I get struck by an errant globe flying out of this man's face. I just stood entranced by his grotesque appearance.

The bleeding inside of his head, most likely from a ruptured aneurysm, was dangerously close to causing his brain to herniate. This means that since there was nowhere for the pressure inside his head to release, it would cause the brain to squeeze through the small hole at the base of his skull, called the foramen magnum, killing the patient. Imagine holding a peach-size water balloon in your hand, squeezing it, and then watching part of the balloon pop between the circle formed by your thumb and finger. You get the idea. Balloons don't mind such treatment; brains, on the other hand . . .

"Have you done a ventriculostomy before . . . *sllllrrrrrppppp?*"

Pratt's question snapped me out of my trance. "Um . . ." I took a breath. "I've seen a few."

I lied. I had never seen any. But the rule of thumb in residency training is that you never directly admit to never having done a procedure, and you certainly never admit to never having seen one. Since the rule of thumb in training is "See one, do one, teach one," if you ever want to actually do a procedure, then you just need to get your hands wet. So I lied.

"Good . . . *sllllrrrrrppp* . . . so you can do this one." Pratt seemed pleased.

The problem was, I did not want to do this procedure! I have no idea why I automatically lied to him. Maybe it was that it was ingrained in me as a resident to train and do procedures that I automatically lied. But this, this was something different entirely. A ventriculostomy, for lack of a better word, is basically drilling a hole in this man's head to let the pressure off. With all due respect to the trusted pioneers in the field of neurosurgical science, that is basically what it is.

"*Slllllrrrrrpppp* . . . come on up to the head of the bed and get gloved up."

Oh my god, I thought. *He's serious! He wants me to do this procedure!*

I eased around to the head of the bed and stepped up on the small step stool that the nurse had intuitively known we would need and donned a pair of sterile gloves. Pratt was on my right and would hand me instruments and instruct me through the procedure. Above his head, hanging on the wall, was a light box that illuminated the patient's CT brain scan. I stared at the image long enough to see bright blood in areas of the brain where there should not be blood and had just enough medical knowledge to know that that was not good. I returned my attention to the top of the patient's head that had been prepped and draped for the procedure.

Then I prayed. Silently. I think I really prayed for the first time in my life.

Pratt reached down onto the table of sterile instruments before us and, with very unsteady fingers, handed me a scalpel. I had to make my hand match the snakelike movements of his in order to even grasp the instrument. And in a flash, just then, it became clear to me exactly why I was doing this procedure: because he can't! He wasn't offering to teach me the procedure out of kindness—he needed me to do it.

My pulse raced even faster, and I began to feel sweat bead on my forehead.

"Use the blade . . . *slllrrrppppp* . . . and poke a hole through the skin down to his skull . . . *slllrrrrpppp*," he said as he pointed to an area on top of this poor patient's head. I took the pointed scalped and pushed it through the skin deeply until the tip of the blade met the resistance of bone and withdrew the blade. Blood began oozing out of the hole and cascading slowly down behind his ear and down his neck.

I handed the scalpel back to Pratt, and as he took it, he replaced it with another instrument, something I had never seen before. With a quick slapping motion, he handed what looked like an eggbeater! Not the handheld whisk tool like my grandmother used to prepare eggs in the kitchen, but something like the mechanical device with a circular hand crank that, when turned, would, through a series of gears, rotate two interlocked beaters that would work in tandem to whip the eggs. But instead of two beaters, this finely tooled surgical instrument had a two-inch-long drill bit on the end!

With the left hand holding the body of the instrument, which was about the size and shape of an avocado, the right hand turned the small crank on its side, which, in turn, rotated the drill bit.

"Put the drill into the hole . . . *slllrrppp* . . . you just made," Pratt instructed. As I did this, he placed his hand on top of the instrument as well. Looking over his left shoulder at the two dimensional images of this man's brain hanging on the light box, I could see in his face. He was making mental calculations. He began guiding the trajectory of the drill much like he was making minute adjustments with a joystick. When it looked like he was satisfied, he took his hand off mine and said, "OK, Cole, drill."

I swallowed hard. With my hands frozen in place, doing my best to hold the angle of approach that Stringer had just visualized, my mind raced.

This is wrong, I thought to myself.

No, you have to do this, I answered myself. My brain began having a conversation with itself.

I can't drill a hole in this man's brain!

If you don't, he will die.
He needs a doctor!
You are the doctor.

"What's wrong, Cole?" Pratt's question broke into my mental argument.

"Nothing," I answered. Intuitively, I knew that showing hesitation as a member of the surgical trauma service was an unspoken cardinal sin. When seconds could mean the difference between life and death, you do not hesitate. "I'm OK."

Slowly, I began to turn the handle of the drill. Nothing happened. "*Slllrrrpppp* . . . push down hard," Pratt instructed. I did. I pushed the tip of the bit hard into the bone underneath, and my heart raced even harder. The drill bit began to find purchase, and I could feel the resistance as the metal started to bite into bone.

"Stop!"

My throat seized shut at the sound of Pratt's voice. He reached up and made a minute adjustment to the trajectory of the drill while looking over his shoulder at the patient's scan. "OK, go," he said.

Again, I started turning the crank of the drill. Small bits of bone and blood began to fill the spiral clefts of the drill bit, rising up and out of the hole as if on a spiral escalator. The drill bit slowly disappeared into his skull for what seemed like an unimaginable depth. Down. My hand was beginning to get tired. Down. Blood and bone continued exiting up and out around the bit. Down. Down. Down. *Pop!* The drill bit suddenly gave way as it exited the underside of his skull, and I intuitively stopped turning lest it plunge into the soft brain tissue underneath.

"Did you feel that?" Pratt asked.

I shook my head yes.

"OK . . . *slllrrrppp* . . . reverse the drill and take it out." I did as he said, trembling. I knew he could see how nervous I was, and I silently cursed myself for my emotion. I gave the drill to him, and he handed me a catheter that resembled a long thin rigid straw.

"OK . . . *sllrrrrpppp* . . . thread this through the hole and keep pushing it in until you get to the lateral ventricle." The ventricles of the brain are empty spaces, and I knew that this was to be the eventual resting place for the tip of the catheter in order to relieve the pressure that was killing our patient. I slid the catheter through the dense wet sponge of the brain bit by bit, watching it disappear into the depths of his head. Suddenly blood began to pour out of the free end of the catheter.

"You got it!" Pratt said with elation. "Good job . . . *slllrrrppp.*"

I took the first real breath I had taken since this ordeal had begun and let it out slowly. The air came out in staccato bursts due to the hammering of my heart, and I was again embarrassed at the outward sign of my anxiety. I let my gaze drift away from the patient's scalp and toward Pratt, who was smiling. Although due to his injury not all the muscles of his face coordinated, the parts that did stretched his mouth into a broad grin. And I smiled back.

The machines that had been monitoring the patient's vital signs since we came into the room began to register readings that indicated an improvement in the patient's condition. This was a promising sign that we had done everything right and that our patient might live. I felt my shoulder muscles, which had been tense with fear, relax a little.

After the procedure, I went back to the call room and slept. I slept hard.

When I awoke the next morning, because the hydrocodone was wearing off or by natural forces, I sat bolt upright in bed. I was surprised I had been allowed to sleep that long. On the trauma service, it was not uncommon to either get no sleep or to be awakened so many times by the trauma pager I might as well not have slept. Nonetheless, I felt rested. And I also felt something else. It was hard to put my finger on exactly what it was.

My thoughts returned to the night previous and everything that had transpired during that harrowing procedure. Although commonplace, it was the first time that I myself had done a ventriculostomy. It might have been the first time that, as a direct result of my actions, I had saved a life! Maybe what I was feeling was pride. Maybe it was self-confidence. I don't know, but whatever it was, it felt good, and feeling good about myself was unfamiliar to me. I smiled a little and began to think that all the pain in my life and all the misery had led up to something. Thinking about what I had done gave me a sense that suddenly . . . just maybe . . . there was a purpose in it all.

I caught a glimpse of the amber-colored bottle of hydrocodone sitting on the small bedside table next to the phone. For the first time in a long time, I didn't instinctively reach for it. *Maybe for today,* I thought, *just for today, I don't need it.* That felt good.

Instead, I reached for the phone beside the bottle and dialed Pratt's cell number. He picked up.

"Cole . . . *slllrrrppp* . . . great job last night,"

"Thank you." I beamed. "That was an awesome procedure."

"Yep. It went really well," he replied. There was a long pause, where I didn't really know what else to say. He broke the silence. "Well, I gotta go . . . *slllrrrppp* . . . I will see you later at grand rounds."

"OK, I'll see you later." I started to hang up the phone but pulled it back to my ear. "Pratt?"

"Yeah?" he answered.

"How did the patient do?"

"Oh, he died," he answered nonchalantly. "I'll see you in a little while . . . *slllrrrppp.*" He hung up.

I sat shocked for a long time holding the receiver to my ear. When I finally replaced it on the cradle, I saw the bottle of hydrocodone syrup again. Instinctively, I grabbed it. I pushed down on the cap and turned. I removed it, put the bottle to my lips, and drained the remaining liquid into my mouth, swallowing frantically.

Before joining Pratt at grand rounds, I briefly detoured to 4 East.

Beverly, the patient I had assisted during her gastric bypass surgery, would have been transferred here.

Before I entered her room, I could see through the cracked door that it was dark inside. After an obligatory short knock, I entered the room and switched on the light. It would seem to me that parents and members of the medical field are the only groups of people who are socially allowed to wake people up in such a rude fashion. Try this in any other situation, and you are likely to be met with a stream of profanity from the other person. In the hospital, it was an expected and begrudgingly endured practice.

Beverly woke up slowly, still groggy from the surgery, and rolled over in my direction.

"Hi," I said softly. "How are you?"

It was only after I got closer to the bed that I noticed someone else in the room.

Lying on the foldout couch beside Beverly's bed was a child who looked to be about ten or eleven years old. Looking as if she was waking up the fastest, I spoke to her first.

"Hi, who are you?" I said in my practiced high-pitched I'm-talking-to-a-child voice.

"I'm Olivia," she replied sleepily. "That's my mom," she continued, using one hand to point to Beverly and the other to rub her eyes as she sat up. "Are you her doctor?"

Instinctively, I looked over my shoulder to see if a doctor had followed me into the room. Realizing she was actually talking to me, I answered, a little embarrassed, "Yes, I'm one of them."

"Are you going to take care of my mom?" Olivia asked as she looked at me expectantly.

I just stood there.

It was a straightforward question and cut right to the heart of my anxiety as a newly deemed doctor.

It was as if the word *yes* was paralyzed nervously on the tip of my tongue. It just sat there in the same way a shy fat kid would stand at the end of a diving board for the first time, his arms unconsciously covering his chubby torso from the gaze of the other children and him staring down at the water. Much like he wanted to jump, I wanted to confidently say, "Yes, I will take care of your mom, Olivia. Don't you worry about a thing."

What eventually came out was, "I am one of the people who will look after your mom."

Olivia seemed to only partially accept the answer by saying "OK," lying back down with her back to me, and covering up with her hospital-issue blanket. An act that basically said, "OK, whatever."

Disappointed in myself for my apparent lack of command presence, I sighed. Children have an inborn bullshit meter. Advancing adulthood, however, seems to dull its precision. It's almost as if we, as humans, become less attune to reality the more full of shit we become ourselves. But Olivia, still grounded in the reality of youth, saw straight through me.

As I returned my attention back to Beverly lying in front of me on the hospital bed, I could see she had gone back to sleep.

Turning the light off, I retreated, figuratively and literally, out of the room. After all, I was late for grand rounds.

Disastrous Bypass

Did you know something surprising that weighs eight hundred pounds? Whale testicles. And that's not the *combined* weight either. No, *each* testicle weighs roughly eight hundred pounds.

Did you know that in 1840, Queen Victoria was presented with an eight-hundred-pound cheddar cheese wheel as a wedding gift?

Do you know something else that may surprise you can weigh eight hundred pounds? A human being.

As an intern on the general surgery service, it was my job to take care of the patients who had bariatric surgery in the hospital. If you are unfamiliar with the gastric bypass procedure, please allow me a few moments to enlighten you.

Humans are unique in many ways. One of those ways is that they can develop a degree of obesity that renders them literally incapable of caring for themselves. They become unable to walk or even stand. Any type of exercise becomes impossible, and they become unable to even care for themselves. Clothing is not made in their size, and even if they were physically capable of clothing themselves, they couldn't.

Even sleep becomes an impossible task. Yes, you heard me correctly: sleep is impossible. Not only do people gain weight in their external bodies, but their internal bodies get fat. The upper airway in obese patients closes off from the surrounding fat and becomes so dangerously narrow that when they sleep, it closes off completely. Imagine that our patient is a donut (sorry for the fat-food analogy) and the hole in the donut is their airway. As the donut-patient gets larger and larger, the hole of the donut gets smaller and smaller. Ultimately, it becomes so small that when the patient falls asleep and the tongue relaxes into the back of the mouth, it closes off the airway completely. When this happens, their unoxygenated brain sends out an internal alarm mechanism that wakes the patient up seconds before they die. This cycle of falling asleep, waking up, falling asleep, waking up occurs hundreds of times throughout the night, effectively rendering the person a functional insomniac.

So even if our obese patient wanted to lose weight at this point in their life, they would have neither the mobility nor energy to do so. But fear not! Medical science, in its infinite wisdom, has delivered its idea of a cure. It's called gastric bypass surgery.

The surgery involves opening the patient's abdominal cavity, stapling a portion of the stomach shut, and thereby rendering it capable of accepting only a fractionally smaller portion of food at any given meal. The intestines are then cut and rerouted to accommodate for the smaller portions. Thus, instead of the person having to work off calories, surgically they are literally restricted as to how much food they can ingest.

Sounds great in theory, doesn't it? And it does, in fact, prove successful if the patient survives the recovery from surgery. That is a very big *if*! The patients who undergo this type of procedure sometimes do very well. Ironically, the less weight the person goes into the procedure with, the better they do. But the heavier the patients, the worse they do.

A host of postoperative complications plague the more obese patients, such as respiratory infections, skin infections, blood clots, kidney failure, heart failure, and skin ulcers, just to name a few.

The surgical ICU had quieted down after morning visiting hours were over. Distraught family members, many of whom lived like refugees in the waiting room, had finally filed out. I stood at the nurses' station sipping acrid, stale coffee out of the largest Styrofoam cup I had been able to find and looked out across the expanse of open bays. The curtains had been pulled back to expose dozens of postoperative gastric bypass patients in various stages of disrepair. Some were doing very well, but some . . .

Ms. Amy was one of my favorite patients but was back in the ICU again. She had returned home after her surgery and accidentally given herself a third-degree burn on her abdomen. She had fallen asleep with a heating pad on her stomach. When I say *stomach*, that is not quite true. What she had done was shoved the electric heating pad under the massive fold produced by her belly fat that draped almost to her midthigh when she was standing. While on the strong pain medications, she had been unaware that the heating pad was literally cooking through her skin and fat. Upon returning to the hospital, more surgery, called debridement, was required to remove the charred tissue around the burn. It left her with a hole in her groin and belly roughly the size and depth of a child's lunch box.

In the room next to hers was Mr. Randall's. Mr. Randall had been in the ICU for almost four months. He was eight hundred pounds. He had suffered nearly every complication possible after his bypass surgery and was not improving. He was being kept alive on a ventilator and being fed through his IV and also a tube that had been inserted into his stomach. He was in kidney failure and received routine dialysis. He was being kept in a medically assisted coma to ensure he did not wake up and attempt to tear the ventilator tube out of his throat.

"Are you ready?" asked the nurse.

I had been so engrossed in thought that I had not even noticed the nurse standing at his bedside who had asked/yelled the question to me.

My heart sank a little as I realized *what* she had asked me. It was time to debride Mr. Randall's decubitus ulcer.

I set down my Styrofoam cup and removed my white coat and draped it over the back of a chair. As I walked toward his room, I didn't know what I was dreading more: working on Mr. Randall or dealing with his nurse Sheila.

Sheila was standing at his bedside, looking at me with arms folded, and wearing a look of impatient indignation. She was regarded in the ICU as not only the most skilled nurse but also the most feared by residents. Although diminutive in size standing next to the bed holding Mr. Randall, her reputation as having an "eat residents for lunch" attitude somehow made her dwarf him in comparison.

Sheila's reputation was not her only imposing feature; so was her physical appearance. She was a redbone mulatto built for the demanding physical work of a surgical ICU. With a frame that would be equally suited for roller derby or work on the road hoisting lights and speaker equipment for the Lilith Fair, she waited for me. I walked over smiling as best I could.

"C'mon, Cole," she said. "Let's get this over with so you can get busy doing nothing again."

I smiled and said, "Good morning to you too, Sheila."

She rolled her eyes and motioned with her head. "Get on the other side of the bed and help me roll him."

Mr. Randall would have to be on his side to perform the debridement on his decubitus ulcer. A decubitus ulcer is a wound that can occur when patients are lying on their back too long. Typically they show up at the top of their ass where the cheeks come together, and they are roughly the size of a quarter on the small side and a hamburger bun on the large side. But that's in a normal-size patient, and Mr. Randall was *not* a normal-size patient.

As Sheila grabbed an arm and a leg from her side of the bed and I pushed from my side to roll Mr. Randall on his right side, he began to move. Slowly at first, but then with more momentum, he turned. IV tubing, ventilator hoses, urine catheters, and feeding lines all had to be monitored lest they be ripped from their corresponding orifices.

As I pushed, the great expanse of his back began to emerge, revealing a hot, fetid landscape of skin and human secretions. Heat and the smell of human excrement hit me hard as I pushed. I looked up at Sheila on the other side of the bed as she pulled not because she was pleasing to look at but simply to pull my face away from the smell.

I saw she was smiling at me!

Not pleasantly or admirably, but with assured self-satisfaction. Seasoned nurses always knew small details of their job that makes them more tolerable and the job of the resident a little less so. Knowing which side of the patient to be on when you roll them is one of those details. With her face and mouth safely out of aroma range, mine were squarely in the midst of it!

While continuing to hold my breath, I kept pushing and smiled back at her.

When we both innately sensed that Mr. Randall was at a balance point on his side, we let go and stepped back.

The vast expanse of his back resembled a mural of human horrors. The back of his head and hair were caked with dried sputum and snot that had leaked around from the tracheostomy tube in his neck. Fat folds, which only intermittently saw the light of day, were filled with a paste-like material produced when sweat mixes with sloughing skin that resembled grainy Elmer's glue. Liquid stool, impossible to contain even under the best circumstances, had wicked up through the bedsheets and adhered to the hair on his back, giving the entire dermal landscape a brown stucco appearance.

And then there was the decubitus ulcer!

Calling it an ulcer was only appropriate because we had no other word in medical terminology that did it justice. It was technically an ulcer in the same way that Australia is technically an island.

No matter how many times over the last few weeks that I saw it, it always struck me as to just how impossible it should be that someone could be alive with this type of wound.

Extending from the small of his back to well below where his buttocks *should* have been was a hole roughly the size of a manhole cover! He simply no longer had an ass. It had been cored out, and only empty space remained. And if the sheer diameter of the wound were not disturbingly impressive enough, it was the depth of the wound that was most alarming. Moving from the surface down, it extended past the skin, down through fat, and past the muscle tissue. The side walls of the huge crater resembled the geographical cross sections of the planet Earth from elementary school, but instead of crust-mantle-core, it would have been labeled skin-fat-muscle.

At its bottommost depth and covering the entire floor of the wound were the bones of his pelvis! I was casually looking at deep areas of the human anatomy that should never be exposed to the human eye, and it was somehow OK.

Sheila had, by this time, come around to my side of the bed and was standing next to the sterile surgical tray that she had set up at Mr. Randall's bedside long before she had ever summoned me.

"You ready to get this done?" she asked with the usual low level of annoyance in her tone that nurses saved only for interns. "He's not my only patient," she stated with punctuated resentment. But despite her barely palpable level of continuous hostility toward interns, if my ass was falling off and I needed snatching back from the jaws of death, there was no other nurse I would pick to be mine other than Sheila. I never told her this—maybe I should have.

I donned a pair of sterile gloves and picked up a scalpel and forceps. I started carving away tissue from the edges of the wound and laying the pieces aside. It was necessary to remove dead and rotting tissue since after the tissue died and lost its blood supply, it began to grow dangerous bacteria that, if allowed to reach the blood supply, could kill the patient and cause sepsis. And since this wound was periodically being flooded with the patient's own stool, it was just that much more important to keep it as clean as humanly possible.

After a few minutes of just watching me (and I believe telepathically wishing me ill will), Sheila broke the silence. "Are you OK on your own with this?" she asked as she took off her own gloves, which meant "I'm leaving whether it's OK or not."

"Yeah," I answered. "I got this." But I was already speaking to her back as she walked out of the room. "Thank you." I don't know if she even heard me.

With that, I was left to my own thoughts as I snipped away tissue from the gaping crater in Mr. Randall's back.

(Snip snip.)

I wonder if Mr. Randall will make it out of this ICU?

(Snip snip.)

Probably not.

(Snip snip.)

Jesus, he's been in this little room for four months. Unconscious. Does he know what's going on?

(Snip snip.)

If he did know, do you think he would want us to stop? Or keep doing everything we are doing to him?

(Snip snip.)

If I keep taking drugs like I do, am I going to end up overdosed on a ventilator just like him?

"CODE 99 . . . 4 EAST!"

The automated voice over the hospital PA broke me out of my internal dialogue. A patient was crashing on the med/surg ward, and a call was made for all available doctors to report to that floor. In other words, some bad shit was going down. I peeled off the sterile gloves and headed to 4 East.

After sprinting up all four flights of stairs in what felt like eight or ten strides, I arrived on 4 East. I easily spotted the normal commotion that accompanies a code in the hospital. Outside the door leading into one of the many room lining the halls were nonessential medical personnel peering into its depths. Arms folded and looking very concerned, they nervously peered up and down the hall, waiting for someone who knew what the hell they were doing to arrive. Their faces relaxed a little seeing me heading their way.

Clearly they didn't understand that just because I was wearing scrubs and a stethoscope draped around my neck did not necessarily mean I knew what the hell I was doing. Technically I was only qualified to be medical slave labor, with just enough knowledge to do a tremendous amount of damage if not properly supervised.

As I neared the room, my heart began to sink with recognition. I had been here this morning. This was Beverly's room.

I quickly remembered Olivia, Beverly's daughter, and her simple straightforward question, "Are you going to take care of my mother?"

I remembered too my evasive answer; how I had stammered and sputtered, unassured.

As I pushed past the throng of onlookers outside the room, I thought, *Well, Olivia, we are about to find out.*

Beverly was seated on the side of her hospital bed and leaning forward with her hands on her knees. Oxygen tubing, which ran from her nose, and IV lines intertwined with heart-monitoring cables and resembled vines encircling her body. I had never seen her awake and was shocked by her appearance. Her previously brown skin was now ashen gray, and as she looked up at me, her pupils were wide black pools of fear. Her breathing was far too rapid and shallow, and she could only speak to me in short bursts between respirations.

"I . . . can't . . . breath . . ." she barely managed to say.

I quickly scanned the room for help. There was no one.

Her nurse, who had been quickly on my heels pushing the crash cart, came into the room almost knocking me over with it. "Move it or lose it, Dr. Cole," she said as she pulled the large critical care cart to a halt beside me. It resembled a large toolbox on caster wheels, and point in fact, that's exactly what it was. When she leaned back to bring the hulking cart to a stop, she accentuated the maneuver by saying, "We need to intubate her now!"

It was then I heard the soft weeping from the other side of the room. Olivia was watching the whole scene through streaming tears. She was still in the foldout bed I had seen her in earlier that morning. Clutching her blanket in front of her, her eyes were fixed in terror on her mother.

I looked back at Beverly, and something switched in me.

All that had been in me previous to this moment left. The fear, the uncertainty, the shyness—all left in an instant. Everything thing that was Kiffer was gone, and the only thing that remained was everything Dr. Cole had learned about medicine in the last four years of training.

"You're right," I replied to the nurse. And in one swift motion, I unlocked the wheels to Beverly's hospital bed with the foot-lever mechanism, gripped the footboard, and pulled both Beverly and her bed away from the wall at the head of her bed to make room.

I leaped into the space created between the headboard and the wall. Pulling the removable headboard up in one swift motion, it slid on its rails and came off in one smooth motion. Almost in unison upon its removal, Beverly lost consciousness. She fell to her side, and grabbing beneath both shoulders, I pulled her onto her back in preparation for the intubation of the endotracheal tube. I could feel from the hard tremors in her muscles she was seizing.

"Push one hundred milligrams of succinylcholine now!" I barked to the nurse, who immediately began retrieving the medication from the crash cart.

I pulled on a pair of latex gloves and began positioning Beverly's head from behind to gain access to her airway. Placing my hands on either side of her head, I tilted it backward and up in the textbook sniffing position I had seen done hundreds of times during other intubations. Placing a bag ventilator mask over her mouth and nose, I used one hand to seal the mask over her face and the other to squeeze the oxygenated air into her lungs manually.

As I stood ventilating her and waiting for the paralyzing agent the nurse was administering in her IV to take effect, I again looked around the room. Other resident doctors, more experienced than me, had filtered into the room and were watching me now. Although they looked relaxed, I knew they were standing at ready to take over should I screw this up in the least.

Another nurse was now escorting Olivia out of the room. She was still crying as the nurse took her hand and led her out into the hallway. I saw her give one last tearful look over her shoulder at me before disappearing through the door.

I could feel Beverly's muscles begin to relax through my grip on her head. I knew it was time to do this now. Literally, there was no going back. In order to effectively place her endotracheal tube, I had used a paralyzing drug that rendered every muscle in her body flaccid, including her diaphragm. She was no longer breathing at all on her own. I had to move fast now.

Removing the mask, I grabbed the curved laryngoscope blade the nurse had placed beside her head. The blade is a battery-operated device that resembles a small sickle with a light on the end that, when properly inserted, will reveal the patient's vocal cords, the target entrance for the breathing tube.

Using my free hand, I opened Beverly's mouth and slipped the curved metal blade past her teeth and over her tongue. Pulling up with the handle, her entire head lifted off the mattress, and as I bent down to peer into her throat, I could see nothing but spit and regurgitated stomach contents in her mouth. *Damn!* I thought.

"Suction," I called to the nurse, holding my free hand in the air. In it she slapped the end of the suction device. I slipped the suction catheter into the debris of her mouth, and it slurped and vacuumed. Bloody brown liquid and chunks rose out of her throat and up and out through the tubing. Removing the catheter, I again peered down in the open lifeless mouth and I saw them—the vocal chords.

"Endotracheal tube," I again barked orders to the nurse, never taking my eyes off the intended target.

The nurse placed the long rigid tube in my open hand. I pushed the end of the tube past and through the pearly-white chords and removed the laryngoscope in one fluid motion. I reattached the ventilator bag to the free end of the tube that was protruding out of her mouth and squeezed.

Pratt Singer, whom I was unaware had even been one of the other residents in the room, leaned over the bed and placed his stethoscope on her chest. He listened over both lungs as I squeezed the bag and watched her chest rise and fall.

"I think you got it, Cole . . . *slrrrrp*," he said, followed with his trademark crooked smile.

The Art of the Slow Code

Before becoming a physician, it was all I ever wanted to be. I would envision myself scurrying around some imagined busy ER and snatching people back from the grips of an untimely death. I saw myself telling family members of how, as a result of the heroics of our medical team, their loved ones would again be around to spend happy days with them. I saw death as an unnatural act, greedily and insatiably devouring unsuspecting victims far too soon in their life, and it had to be usurped at all costs, lest it be allowed to devour the innocence of life.

I saw saving a life as the ultimate of services. I saw life as all and everything, and that without it, nothing existed.

I know today that this is not true, not entirely anyway.

What changed my mind? What turned things on its head and allowed me to accept death as a natural progression of life? The answer had been long in coming and was quite unsuspected. It was not so much that I stopped seeing death as the ultimate nemesis to human life; rather, I began to see something else as a far greater and more devastating adversary: human suffering.

Suffering, clothed in every imaginable disguise and rationalized in the most devious delusions, is our truest ailment. Driven by fear and perceived lack, human suffering is the truest death. It occurs in our quiet moments. It is the phantom voice inside our own thinking mind that, without ceasing, whispers its horrors into our heart. Suffering is the magician, the illusionist we have an unfailing belief in that life could somehow be better. That whatever exists in our life is somehow not right—not big enough, not beautiful enough, not thin enough, not *anything* enough. And in attempt to make our life enough, we suffer. And in the self-inflicted crusade to find enough, we find suffering. We find it under every overturned stone, behind every drawn heavy curtain, and in the eyes of every lover we have silently begged to make us complete. In no outstretched grasping hand or at the end of an extended accusatory finger do we find the source of our suffering, but only in the ceaseless longing inside ourselves do we find the truest source of our pain.

For Beverly, the search for happiness would soon be over.

After her successful intubation, she was transferred to the ICU. I did not immediately follow the throngs of people who accompanied her down to her new room.

Instead, I went in search of my own phantom peace. The burgeoning of withdrawal was ever present. I made a detour to my call room and rummaged through my bag for a bottle of morphine. Removing the amber bottle from my bag, I made a mental note of how many pills I had remaining before shaking out four into my hand. Two of the small brown pills, I swallowed, while the other two I crushed with my back molars and allowed the chalky contents to coat the inside of my mouth to absorb faster. I sat on the side of the bed and thought about what had just happened. It had been my first successful unassisted intubation, and

I was proud. Like the drug that was now leaking into my bloodstream, the thought of having momentarily saved her life fulfilled me. The thought gave me outward purpose, enlarging me, inflating a false sense of who I was and my place in the world. I remembered the other residents, the nurses, and the respiratory technicians who had been watching me, and I felt important. I felt expanded.

The days that followed changed me. As if in Beverly's suffering, I saw the truth of life, and in her death, the truth of suffering.

Day One

In the ICU, nurses were scurrying to place heart monitors on Beverly's chest. Respiratory technicians attached her breathing tube to the ventilator, which would serve as her mechanical lungs. She had not regained consciousness yet. I watched from outside the room at the insect-like coordination of care that took place, a multitude of people working effortlessly in unison without any sign of outward communication.

Sheila, who was also Mr. Randall's nurse, would being taking care of Beverly today.

"What happened upstairs, Dr. Cole?" she asked me, coming out of the room.

"We don't know," I said. "She had gastric bypass yesterday and was doing well after surgery. Then this morning, she just crumped."

Crumping is the word we used to describe all variation of shit hitting the fan. Until we knew exactly what caused her to go downhill, we simply said the patient *crumped.*

"Well . . ." Sheila said, looking over her shoulder toward Beverly's and then back at me, "at least make yourself useful and put in her central line."

I could see that Sheila had already set up for the procedure, and from her tone, she needed me to get busy on it. A central line is a deeper IV than the ones we typically place in patient's arms and hands.

After taking off my white coat, I draped it on the back of the chair I had been sitting in and headed into the room. Beverly's eyes were closed, and I focused my attention on the area of exposed skin below her right collarbone. Using Betadine to cleanse the skin and then pulling on a sterile set of latex gloves, I set to work.

Picking up a large syringe from the sterile tray that more resembled a turkey baster than a surgical instrument, I attached a needle that was approximately six inches in length and the diameter of a coffee straw. I plunged the needle into the skin below her collarbone and aimed for the notch just above the breast bone. As the megasized needle entered the skin, Beverly didn't flinch. I guided the needle underneath the bone all the while pulling back on the plunger of the syringe to create negative pressure inside the barrel. The needle continued its decent into her upper chest until it hit its desired target, the subclavian vein, heralded by the filling of dark unoxygenated blood into the barrel of the syringe. Twisting off the barrel and leaving the bevel end of the syringe jutting out of the skin, blood began spilling out onto her chest. Quickly I took a long metal wire and began threading it into the exposed end of the needle. Inch by inch, I threaded the wire through the inner lumen of the needle as it disappeared into her body.

As I pushed the wire into her vein, I turned my attention to her heart monitor above her head, which registered every beat. As soon as it became erratic and registering extra beats, I knew the wire had come to rest in its correct location: the right ventricle of her heart. Pulling back now to remove the tip of the wire out of her heart, I then removed the needle from her skin, leaving only the wire that now marked the course from the outside world into her deep subclavian vein. I then grabbed the long IV catheter from the sterile tray. Placing the tip of the wire into the hollow tip of the catheter, I threaded the catheter into her vein and then removed the wire through the lumen of her now successfully placed central line IV.

The entire procedure took less than ten minutes, and when it was through, I sutured the exposed end of the catheter to her skin with a long straight sewing needle. Not once during the entire process did Beverly show any signs of feeling what I was doing. This was not a good sign.

Day 2

All manner of testing had been initiated to discover what had happened to Beverly. Nothing was revealing any answers:

> EKG: negative for heart attack
> Brain MRI: negative for strokes
> Lung CT Scans: negative for clots in the lungs
> EEG: negative for seizure activity
> Blood Tests: negative for metabolic causes
> Negative, negative, negative.

Day 7

Strong medications called vasopressors were being administered to keep Beverly's blood pressure high enough to sustain life. She was requiring daily resuscitation when her heart would quit beating. Spontaneous lethal cardiac electrical activity would be met with countless rounds of external defibrillations delivered through electrical pads placed on her chest.

During that first week in the ICU, specialist physicians had been consulted to render their opinion on her care and to offer any assistance they could give:

> Cardiology: no recommendations
> Pulmonary: no recommendations
> Infectious Disease: no recommendations
> Neurology: no recommendations

Day 14

There is a back door into the ICU. Most doctors and nurses would come through the rear stairwell and descend into its depths through this back entrance. They did this not for convenience but to avoid the front entrance at all costs. For outside the electronically secure front entrance was the family waiting room.

The waiting room for the ICU resembled a refugee camp. Family members who had loved ones in the ICU stayed in a perpetual state of unease, fear, and insomnia. ICU stays could range in the order of days to months, and family members were allowed back only during certain hours of the day. For this reason, the waiting room perpetually took on the appearance of suffering. Like the overbooked passengers awaiting flights in airport gates, families set up "homes" in every corner of the room. Bed palates made of dirty clothing were strewn about the floor, crudely constructed hammocks made of sheets would be stretched between chairs for children to sleep in, and half-eaten cafeteria food littered the spaces on the floor not occupied by living people. Security would routinely be called on Hispanic families, who, due to cultural differences, didn't comprehend that although food can be *consumed* in the waiting room, it cannot however be *prepared* there. Hot plates, Bunsen burners, and Crock-Pots would routinely need to be confiscated, and interpreters would be used to explain why this was a safety hazard.

When one of the medical staff in the hospital walked past this area, they could herald an oncoming ambush if recognized. As if on unspoken cue, unshaven faces and heads with unkempt hair would pop up and out of man-made tents or away from the television to train eyes on whoever was approaching wearing scrubs or a hospital ID. Faces, with eyebrows raised and mouths agape, would swivel in unison toward any oncoming personnel. The desperation from these faces was almost unbearable to witness. Most of the family—who would have most certainly traded places with their sick father, mother, or God forbid, child—were simply anguished for any good news.

It was into this environment that I had been elected to go and speak with Beverly's family.

And the news was not good.

Up to that point, I had only known Olivia, her eleven-year-old daughter. But now, many more family members had joined Olivia in the waiting room, and most of them I had known only as transient human silhouettes at Beverly's bedside during visiting hours. As they saw me approach now, they recognized me as one of the many doctors that had been caring for Beverly. They all rose from chairs and makeshift cots to greet me in the hallway outside the waiting room.

"How is she?"

"Is she waking up?

"When can she come home?"

The questions were coming in rapid-fire succession and without pause from all different sides of me now.

"Hold on," I said, putting a hand up in defense. I could see Olivia standing near the back of the crowd, nestled protectively under an older relative's arm. "I just wanted to update you." I took a deep breath. "Not much has changed with her condition. Unfortunately, now," I paused, meeting as many eyes as I could, "the results of her most recent EEG show that she has no active brain wave activity."

"EE what?" a man from the back interrupted.

"EEG," I corrected him. "It measures the neurological activity of her brain."

"What does that mean?" the questions continued.

"It means that she is," I took another deep breath, "brain dead."

My last statement was met with howls and moans. Two of the women dropped to their knees and immediately began praying.

"I am sorry to be the one to have to tell you this. It's never easy to—" My practiced speech was again interrupted.

"But she's going to be OK, right?"

"So what do you do now?"

"We want to talk to Dr. Carter!"

I unconsciously began to take a step backward as Beverly's family inched closer to me and the waves of their anguish pushed and unbalanced me.

"I am sure Dr. Carter will speak to you, but now we need to talk about changing her status to a Do Not Resuscitate—"

"A Do Not what?"

"It means that if her heart were to stop beating, that we would not use medications or electric shocks to bring her back," I answered one of the men closest to me.

"No! You are going to do everything to save my sister," he said, inching closer and leveling angry eyes to meet mine. I took another unconscious step backward.

Recognizing defeat, I answered, "Of course, sir, absolutely we will." Turning back toward the ICU entrance, I continued, "I will send Dr. Carter to speak with you." My last few words were spoken over my shoulder as I turned in full retreat toward the ICU.

"Don't come back with any more of that bullshit, boy!" I could hear Beverly's brother say as I pressed my security badge to the door sensor and silently prayed it opened quickly. As the magnetized door disengaged, I slid through the opening as soon as it would allow. If I had a tail, it would have been securely tucked between my legs.

As I walked down the hall trying to slow my breathing, Sheila passed on my left.

"How did that go?" she asked.

"Not well," I said without stopping to acknowledge her or her rhetorical question. I could *feel* rather than actually *see* her knowing and experienced, albeit sarcastic, smile. "Not well at all," I said, more to myself, and went to find coffee.

As I walked away, beginning again to lose myself in my own thoughts, Sheila put the punctuation on our brief exchange in the hall.

"It might be time for a slow code."

The comment was said out loud but in a tone that was more appropriate for a thought, barely audible and indecisive, as if the words themselves couldn't decide if they should end in a period or question mark. *What was a slow code?* I thought.

I stopped and turned now to look back at her. She was looking at me now not with her normal-degree mild loathing mixed with impatience but with something different, something deeper, something softer. I would learn later it was a look of compassion, but now it only confused me more.

Without saying another word, she turned and walked away.

Day 21

During the week following my brief exchange with Sheila, Beverly had been resuscitated over nine times.

Powerful drugs had been used to maintain her blood pressures and electric defibrillations to restart her failing heart.

Neurologists had been consulted and had all agreed she was brain dead despite her body's failing efforts to hang on to life.

Her family had refused removal of life-sustaining measures despite the urging of all the medical personnel.

When the monitors began to alarm that she was slipping away from us again, all the ICU medical personnel responded to resuscitate her. But this time would be different.

As I approached her room, the curtains were drawn. And it was quiet.

Had no one from the ICU responded to the call? I thought as I hurriedly pushed the curtain aside to go into the room.

No. Everyone was there. Around her bed were other nurses and respiratory technicians. But no one was frantic. There was not the usual urgency that filled the rooms of other codes that I had been involved in.

Sheila looked up at me as I entered the room.

"Close the curtain, Dr. Cole," she said in a quiet but authoritative voice.

I did as she said, and when I turned around, I could see that all the necessary components were in place for the resuscitation—the code cart, syringes full of medication, cardioversion paddles, everything was in place. But no one was doing anything!

The heart monitor above Beverly's head showed erratic activity. We were losing her.

Had they been waiting on a doctor to start? I thought. No. Most resuscitations started without a physician to lead the code.

Confused, I took the lead as I had seen so many other residents do in the past.

"Start chest compressions," I said in an unhurried even tone, matching the one I had walked into.

"Starting chest compressions," said one of the other nurses in the room. She began slowly pressing on Beverly's chest with slow, shallow thrusts, not the quick deep compressions we were taught to do to maintain circulation, but gentle and slow.

Standing at the foot of Beverly's bed, I looked down. Her feet were exposed, and I could see besides being extremely swollen, her toes were black with necrosis. They had all been reduced to rotting nubs as a side effect of the medicines that had been used over the past three weeks to keep her blood pressure up.

I looked up at her hands, and the tips of all her fingers were in the same condition.

It would seem that despite all our efforts, along with Beverly's brain, her body was dying bit by bit from the outside in.

Looking back up now into the calm faces of all the older and more experienced people around the room, I understood—we were letting her go.

I realized in that moment what they already knew. That even if we were able to resuscitate Beverly this time, or a dozen more times, she was already gone. She was gone three weeks ago. The only thing that hung even to the idea of life were the empty hopes of her family members. I thought of them in the waiting room, their pain, their anguish. How long should they be forced to watch her? Would they, as I had seen so many other families do, dwindle away back to their normal lives, only to intermittently visit Beverly's lifeless body and be forced to relive the horrors week to week, then month to month, then live riddled with guilt at having never visited at all?

I thought too of her daughter, Olivia, and of her simple question, "Are you going to take care of my mother?"

I locked eyes again with Sheila again and nodded slowly to her that I understood. She smiled at me, genuinely and ever so slightly for the first time since I had known her.

I looked back up at Beverly's heart monitor.

"Stop compressions," I said.

The heart monitor was a flat line—asystole.

"Check for a pulse."

The nurse did as I said and shook her head, saying, "No pulse."

I looked at the clock, watching the second hand beat around the face as Beverly's heart had once done.

"Time of death . . . ten thirty-eight," I said.

And it was done.

Rock and Rollover

The morning Beverly died, I tried to kill myself.

Driving home that morning from the hospital, I had been awake for two days straight. Now, for any self-respecting methamphetamine addict, that would be a walk in the park. Since they typically stayed awake for a week or so at a time, it would have been nothing for them to stay up for a couple days. But for me, since my drug of choice was painkillers, it was hard for me to not fall asleep if I stopped moving if for only a moment or two.

Once, Ann had actually found me sleeping in the closet when I had dozed off upright while hanging up my coat. My hand was still suspended in midair gripping the hanger when she had found me. It had been easy to explain away at the time since, after all, I was an intern, and we were expected to live at low levels of exhaustion all the time. Falling asleep while talking to her at dinner, sometimes with a fork in my mouth, had become not the exception but the norm of my life.

So falling asleep while driving was no different.

There was little traffic on the interstate at midday, and as I guided my Toyota Tacoma south toward home, my thoughts drifted back to Beverly. I thought about the short time that I had known her, and saying that I had known her was rather generous indeed. I had watched her young life slip away unceremoniously. I had seen her family endure anguish at her passing, unable to accept the injustice of her death.

Why had she died? I couldn't make sense of it myself. There was no spiritual beauty in her demise. Not that there ever really is in death. I thought about the short amount of time I had spent in churches as a child, when my grandmother had taken me, and of a quote from the apostle Paul:

I have fought the Good Fight. I have finished the race. Finally there is laid up for me the crown of righteousness, which the Lord, the righteous judge, will give to me on that day, and not to me only, but also to all to have loved His appearing.

It made me angry. No offense to Paul, this had just not been my experience of life and death thus far. Where was the righteousness in Beverly's death? Or for any of the other senseless deaths I had witnessed thus far in my career: the overdoses, the gunshot wounds to the head, the suicides, or the deaths of children?

Had any of these people fought the good fight? And if they hadn't, then would there be no reward of righteousness as Paul promised?

As I drove, my mind continued to try and make sense of what I was seeing on a daily basis in the hospital. Months earlier, I had taken care of a six-year-old child with multiple fractures after her mother, a schizophrenic, had intentionally laid her under the tires of the family car and run her over because she was convinced her daughter was possessed with the devil.

Do the mentally ill get handicap status in the fight for the crown of righteousness? I seethed silently, the physical and chemical exhaustion making me angrier. *Do they get a compensatory paper Burger King crown of righteousness?*

And what of her daughter, whom I heard eventually died from her injuries? I guess children get an automatic crown of righteousness being that never got a chance to climb into Paul's spiritual boxing ring and fight the good fight for it anyway.

And who the fuck are we supposed to be fighting anyway?

I caught myself drifting off to sleep.

I shook my head and turned the radio up louder to keep me awake. Listening, but more importantly feeling, the hard rock bass kicks from the speakers behind my seats, I consciously bit down hard on the insides of my cheeks, not enough to draw blood, but enough to let the pain work as an antidote to sleep.

I remembered Mr. Randall too, lying unconscious in a pool of his own excrement in a chemically induced coma. I knew, as everyone else knew, he would never make it out of that hospital. Had he been happy before undergoing his elective procedure to lose weight? *Surely not*, I thought. I imagined him living at home, unable to leave the house because of his size, unable to sleep for more than moments at a time before his oxygen-starved brain forced him back into consciousness so he could breath. Had his endeavor to fight the good fight driven him to the decision to have his surgery? And what of the result? He now laid dying slowly in a hospital cubicle, alone save the intermittent inhumanities forced upon him.

Honk!

Startled awake again by the horn of the car next to me, I realized I had drifted into the lane next to me, coming dangerously close to another car. The driver shot me an angry glance before pulling forward to get ahead of me.

I slapped myself hard in the face and turned the radio up even louder.

Ever-present nausea gripped me. Before leaving the hospital that morning, I had taken two OxyContin. Maintaining the balance was difficult. On one side of the scale sat the ever-looming pain and intolerability of withdrawal, on the other the unconsciousness that came with overdosing myself. Only the smallest window existed in which I could function normally. If I didn't take drugs, I was nonfunctional. If I took too many drugs, I ran the risk of falling asleep and vomiting.

Sudden nausea gripped me.

I had actually learned controlled regurgitation over the years. The doses of narcotics that kept me out of withdrawal usually made me sick. So with learned precision, I reached for the empty soda bottle I kept in the drink holder for just such occasions. Sealing my lips around the edges of the threaded mouth of the bottle and simultaneously venting air through my nose, I regurgitated the entirety of my stomach contents into it. Satisfied the nausea had passed, I took a deep breath in.

Where was the cap? I thought after a halfhearted effort to look for it.

I shrugged and simply replaced the open bottle in the drink holder. I made a mental note to throw it away when I got home, lest I leave any external evidence, in the form of an open container of vomit, of the complete disaster my life really was.

"What about you, Kiffer?" I asked myself out loud now. "Where is the righteousness in your life?"

I had succeeded in the only endeavor in my life: I had become a doctor. I had fulfilled the prophecy of my grandmother so many years ago to become a physician, and what had it amounted to? The success had not resulted in the immediate fulfillment I had expected. I wasn't deliriously happy in being who I was. In fact, I had to take inhuman amounts of narcotics as a reprieve from my own life, a life I had always thought would be complete once I had become Dr. Cole.

But there I was, existing in a constant state of malcontent and self-loathing bitterness. No amount of success had made my soul complete. The real *me* was still unfulfilled. And who was this real me? My entire life had been a never-ending quest, wrought with anxiety-driven purpose, to reach my current destination, and I hated where I was.

This time, I couldn't avoid catastrophe.

I returned to full consciousness just long enough to register the car in front of me was not moving. Stalled in the middle of the interstate, I barreled toward it at over seventy miles per hour and had no hope of stopping!

I jerked the wheel of the Toyota to the left to avoid impacting the car, clipping its left rear bumper instead.

My truck careened to the left. The momentum of the sudden change in direction forced the truck to tip on its rightside tires. Had I been wearing a seat belt, it would surely have cinched me upright in the seat, but as it were, the centripetal force pushed my body down into the passenger side, tearing my hands away from the steering wheel. And just as my life had been figuratively out of control only moments before, so it was now in reality.

Glass shattered as the Toyota toppled over and over.

My body bounced around the interior, slamming uncontrollably into the roof and console of the truck as the contents of the cab swirled around me. The metal of the straining frame and chassis whined for relief from the shearing forces. There was no pain but only shock and fear.

Finally, although it stopped rolling, the truck continued sliding down the interstate on its right side. Bracing myself with my hands and knees on the frame of the door, I could see asphalt passing by through the shattered window only inches from me. Shards of glass and gravel flew up into the cab and past my face as it came grinding to a halt, and then stillness.

Where only moments before had been a cacophony of terrifying sounds, now it gave way to silence. I crouched motionless inside the cab, terrified to move. I remembered the countless mangled and disfigured patients I had seen in the ER since my training had begun, grotesque results and twisted shadows of what they had been only moments before their accidents. *Was I one of them now? Was I headed for the ICU to end up like them?* Panic rose inside me as I pictured myself as one of the patients in my own hospital.

There was no gratitude at being alive, only the fear of living through what had just happened, existing as a pitiful survivor to be cared for as a helpless victim.

As the smell of gasoline and charred rubber filled my lungs, I thought. *People are going to know now. They are going to know about my drug problem.*

I had for years been able to successfully hide all the morose details of what I had become, but now, with this accident, I was going to be found out. Like all the other intoxicated drivers I had seen come through the ER, I would be drug-tested, judged, criticized, and maybe even arrested. I would lose everything I had worked for. I imagined my battered body shackled to the hospital bed, being guarded by sheriff's deputies, awaiting my discharge date to be transported to the jail and await sentencing. My mind began racing for solutions.

I summoned the courage to begin looking at myself for signs of injury. I held up my hands in front of my face; all my fingers were still attached. I consciously began moving my arms and legs, flexing and extending the extremities, and they seemed to be undamaged. *Maybe I am OK*, I thought as a glimmer of hope began to rise in me. I frantically grabbed for the rearview mirror that had broken off during the rollover, took a long deep breath, and looked at my face. Although my hand was trembling, I could still make out all the normal appearances of my face. There were no lacerations, no eye avulsions, and no skull deformities. I opened and closed my jaw, and it seemed to be normal. I took in a deep tremulous breath and let it out as I laid the mirror back down.

Cautiously, I tried to stand up. Grabbing the steering wheel above my head, I hoisted my weight up and spun my legs underneath me. This would be the test. If I had a hip fracture, I knew standing would be impossible. With my feet on the asphalt through the passenger side window, I tenuously began to bear weight, and I stood easily without pain.

My head began to clear as hope arose that I would not end up hopelessly disfigured or paralyzed from the accident.

In the distance, I could hear the faint sound of sirens.

Panic again set in. *I've got drugs in the truck!* My mind strained to remember everywhere they were. I couldn't let narcotics be found in the wreckage. I only had a few seconds before police and ambulances arrived to control the crash site and dispose of anything I had—quick!

I knelt down and opened the glove box, where I kept the methadone. Grabbing the bottle, I poured the remaining pills onto the asphalt and madly began crushing them under my feet, pulverizing them into a fine dust that blended inconspicuously with the broken glass.

Next, I rummaged for my overnight bag and tore open the zipper. Finding the bottle of hydrocodone cough syrup, I twisted off the cap and poured it too onto the ground with the glass and methadone dust. The thick liquid spread out evenly on the ground. I silently hoped it would be sufficiently camouflaged amid the brake and coolant fluid that was also draining from the vehicle as to not raise any suspicions. I shoved the empty bottles into my pockets.

I could tell from the sounds of the sirens and high-pitched whine brakes that the police and ambulances had arrived.

It was time to put on a show. I knew I could not appear injured in any way lest they insist on taking me to the hospital.

Since the shattered front windshield was intact, I had to hoist myself up and out of the cab through the missing driver's side window above my head. Grabbing the frame of the window and being careful not to cut my hands, I put my foot on the steering wheel and, with one swift motion, hefted my weight up and out of the vehicle, landing in a seated position on the doorframe. I lifted my feet up an out of the cab and, with a twisting motion, bounded down from the truck, landing squarely on my feet just in time to see the police officer running toward me.

She stopped in her tracks from a dead run, and I could see she was startled to see me jumping out of the truck.

"Sir, are you OK?" she said, holding up a hand in front of her. "Maybe you should sit down?"

"I'm fine," I said and started to walk toward her.

She took a step back and placed her other unraised hand on the butt of her holstered pistol.

I then realized in my attempt to convince her I was uninjured, I had succeeded only in threatening her. I stopped and held up my hands.

"No, really, I'm fine."

"Just stay where you are for a minute," she said, backpedaling slowly away from me. "I've got to check on these other people."

What other people? I thought, confused.

Over her shoulder, I could see another car about fifty yards back up the interstate. Up to that point, I hadn't even considered what had become of the stalled car I had struck only moments before or that there might have been people inside. She joined the EMTs who had surrounded the other vehicle. Past her retreating frame, I could see four people still inside the car. Although it had sustained only a small amount of damage, the faces I could make out were terrified.

The realization that I hadn't even considered the fact that I might have hurt or even killed anyone else began to set in.

Deep and pervasive self-loathing grew; it grew with emptiness like the tearing open of a wounded portion of my soul. And it spoke.

You never consider anybody but yourself.

Bloated with the darkness of self-criticism, it whispered vacant and load.

You could have killed those people, Kiffer.

More than heard, I felt the words as they infected and maimed my being.

You should be ashamed of yourself.

Tears filled my eyes as I stood and watched the others get out of their car. With the help of the EMTs, each one slowly exited the vehicle. Although I couldn't hear what they were saying, I could see that none of them had been badly injured.

That doesn't matter, Kiffer. You could have killed them!

As tears continued to stream down my cheeks, my legs would no longer hold me. I fell to my knees as if the weight of moment temporarily increased the force gravity around me, pulling me to the earth in the middle of that interstate.

I stayed like that for a long time, watching, crying, being grateful to a god I didn't know for sparing those people's lives and, at the same time, hating him for saving mine.

I knew I had nodded off because of the drugs, and I hated myself.

The police officer started back in my direction. Getting up again, I wiped the tears from my eyes and prepared myself for whatever was going to come next. Would she arrest me? Force me to go to the hospital? I just didn't know at this point and was beginning to think that maybe getting arrested wouldn't be that bad. I was making a fucking mess of what semblance of a life I had, and now it was affecting other people, I a potentially way!

"Sir, are you sure you're OK?" she asked as she got closer to me.

She was a short woman who appeared bulkier than her frame would allow because of the Kevlar vest. Her name tag read Officer Shelly.

"I'm fine, Officer, really." I motioned over her shoulder with a lift of my chin. "Is everybody over there OK?" I tried to sound nonchalant.

"Oh, yes, they're fine." Her voice was reassuring and kind, and I could tell now that she had noticed I'd been crying. I could feel her studying my face as I looked over her shoulder toward the other members of the crash.

After a long silence, she asked, "So what happened here?"

This time I looked her squarely in the eyes. And for a moment, the briefest of moments, I pictured myself saying, "What happened? What happened, you ask? What happened is that I am a hopeless narcotic addict who has no business driving a car or doing anything that requires conscious thought. I shouldn't be trusted behind the wheel. I shouldn't be trusted to be a doctor. Hell, I shouldn't be trusted in your house if you have narcotics because I'll steal them. What happened is, my life is falling into a drug-addicted haze, and I am trying to kill myself . . . How's your day going?"

That was not what I said.

I blinked out of my fantasy and said, "I think they had stalled in the road, and I came up on them too fast to avoid hitting them." I paused for a moment. "I'm just glad they are OK."

Officer Shelly stood and studied me. She had no idea that I had perfected looking *not* high in front of people. Even people like her that should have known better.

"Well, do you think you need to go to the hospital?" She looked me and my scrubs up and down and continued, "It looks like you work in one. I could have the ambulance drive you over there . . ."

"Oh, no, I'm fine really. Just a little bruised up."

She looked at me, then over my shoulder at the mangled truck, and then back at me, perplexed. She raised her eyebrows and, with a slight headshake, said, "OK, well, I guess you could give me a statement, your license, and registration on the way home."

She waited an uncomfortably long time for me to respond. When I didn't, she asked, "You *are* going to need a ride home, right?" motioning back toward the wreckage of my truck.

"Um . . . yes . . ."

When I realized what she was suggesting, that she *not* arrest me, that she *not* take a blood and urine sample at the hospital, and point in fact, actually give me a ride home, I feigned understanding.

"Yes," I continued more confidently, "thank you. I will certainly need a ride home after this."

I had been so focused on not getting arrested or going to the hospital that I had never given any thought to what would happen to me if neither of those things happened. I would have been just as happy to have walked the fifteen miles home at that point.

On the way home, sitting in the passenger seat of the police cruiser and not in the back, I dreaded telling Ann what had happened. She would be asleep when I got there, having worked at the hospital the night before, so I figured I would just tell her when she woke up. I would just let her sleep, I thought.

I was also conscious of sitting on the empty bottle of hydrocodone syrup I had tucked into the back pocket of my scrubs after the accident. Officer Shelly had never searched me, and I had never had an opportunity to get rid of it, so it felt huge and awkward under my right ass cheek during the ride home.

"Thank you, ma'am," I said as we pulled up in front of the apartment and I opened the door of the police cruiser to get out, careful to not have the bottle fall out of my back pocket.

"You be safe," she said as I closed the door.

"I will. Thank you again."

As I watched her pull away and out of the apartment complex, I noticed I also still had the empty bottle of methadone in my front breast pocket. I looked down and read the top of the bottle: Push Down and Turn.

Intervention: Mission Impossible

A couple of weeks after the accident, my mother invited me and Ann to dinner.

"Why do we have to meet her at a hotel near the airport?" Ann asked as she drove us up the interstate. We were in her car (our only car at the moment).

"I don't know," I answered. "She said she wanted to pick up a friend of Tim's who had just flown in from somewhere. I didn't ask."

Tim was my mother's husband. She had remarried shortly after sobering up herself. They had met in AA and had been married for a few years. Although it was her fifth husband, he was the most promising yet. He was sober, and she seemed to love him very much.

"OK," Ann said uneasily after a long sigh. "It just doesn't make any sense, is all. I mean, are we eating at the hotel?"

"I don't know, baby. All she told me was that she wanted me to meet this guy and that he would probably go to dinner with us."

Ann was right. It didn't make a lot of sense. Why couldn't Tim's friend just meet us at the restaurant? Maybe it was because he didn't have a car and didn't want to take a cab? But if that was the case, why didn't Tim just pick him up and take him to the restaurant to meet us?

Ann was pretty accustomed to driving down to my mother's house. We did it a lot. Or she had gotten used to eating alone while I went and ate at my mother's without her. What she didn't know was the real reason I wanted to go there: to steal pills. The majority of my supply came from my mother's methadone. When she wasn't paying attention, I would rummage through her purse or sneak off to her bedroom since I knew where she kept them. I would take what I thought would last at least a few days (it never did) and then sit and talk with her or eat dinner. Recalling those events now brings up a lot of shame for me, but at the time, I saw it as absolutely necessary. If I didn't have those narcotics, I would withdraw, and when that would happen, it didn't just make life difficult—it made it impossible. An inability to sleep, sit still, or even cough without soiling my underwear with diarrhea if I didn't have pills drove me to do things that, when viewed from a sober vantage point, seems unthinkable.

My mother had actually caught me stealing from her once red-handed. A few weeks before the accident, she had walked into the bathroom, where I was stealing one of her fentanyl patches. It used to be a prized find for me since wearing one patch would keep me out of withdrawal for over three days. Not having to worry about stealing pills or writing bad prescriptions for over three days may not sound like much but for me was a vacation from hell.

I used to wear the patch on my left shoulder and then cover the patch with a wide piece of medical tape to conceal the writing on it. When Ann had asked, I told her it was a nicotine patch to stop dipping snuff.

So driving down to see my mother was not at all out of the ordinary. But Ann was right: meeting a stranger at a hotel near the airport was definitely weird.

When we got to the hotel, Tim was waiting on us in the lobby.

"Hi, y'all." Tim stuck out his hand to shake mine and hugged Ann. "C'mon, I want you to meet a friend of mine."

We followed Tim to the elevator, and as we waited, I asked, "Who is this guy?"

"Oh, he's from out of town and won't be here long."

I noticed Tim had avoided answering the question without specifics. When we got on the elevator, I decided to leave it alone. If he didn't want to tell me, that was fine, but this whole scene was getting stranger by the second, and I could sense Ann was nervous too. We stood in silence as the elevator ascended to our floor.

After getting off, we followed Tim down the hall. He stopped at one of the doors and knocked. As we waited for someone to answer, I looked at Tim and could see sweat was beginning to bead up on his forehead.

"Tim," I finally broke the silence, "what's going on here?"

Before he could answer, the door opened. The man standing in the entrance looked to be in his midfifties and heavyset. He was wearing slacks and a sports jacket over a three-button polo.

"Hi, Kiffer," he said as he stuck his hand out to shake mine. "My name is Doug."

After shaking my hand, he turned his attention to Ann and said, "You must be Ann. Hello. I'm glad you could make it too. Please come in and sit down." He stood to the side and allowed us to enter the room.

What I expected to see—twin beds, night stand, TV, and closet—weren't there. Instead, there was a large conference room table in a room much larger than what I expected. But even more confusing than that was the fact that my family was seated around that table. A quick survey around the table was as follows: my youngest brother, Wyatt; my mother, Beverly; my best friend through childhood, Cameron; and the finally, seated in a wheelchair, my grandmother Eunice.

Have you ever had a surprise party thrown for you? And I mean one you really had no idea was coming? Do you remember how it felt? Were you shocked, happy to see all the friends and family you rarely get to see, together all in one place there to celebrate nothing but you? They were probably smiling when you walked in, awkwardly yelling "Surprise!" and then clapping for themselves at having gotten one over on you.

Imagine the same scene now, take away any joy, smiling, or happiness. It was as if someone had thrown me a surprise funeral or maybe a surprise colonoscopy. The only thing missing was the gastroenterologist in the corner of the room snapping on a pair of latex gloves and calling me over, "Kiffer, come on in, hop up on the table. You have been avoiding this for a long time, and your family has hired me to root around in your rectum for a bit. Don't worry, it only hurts if you resist. You're going to feel a little bit of pressure with this . . ."

No one would even look up at me or Ann when we came in.

Closing the door behind us, Doug said, "Please have a seat," and he pointed to two empty chairs at the far side of the table.

"What's going on here?" Ann asked as we made our way to the seats Doug had pointed out.

I made a mental note of two things as we sat down in our preassigned seats: one, Ann had obviously not been told about the intervention, and two, they were putting both of us at the seats farthest from the door. I was already planning my exit strategy.

"Thank you for coming," Doug said as we all took our seats. He adjusted his sports jacket and continued his obviously canned introduction to the proceedings to follow. "Your family has asked me to facilitate today because they have some things they want to say to you. They are worried about you." He met my eyes directly. "We are here today because they love you, Kiffer."

I immediately hated his use of my first name like he knew me. I especially resented the fact that it was part of the practiced speech. I imagined my name being handwritten in some script used thousands of times: "We are here because they love you, _____ (Name of Client)."

The only thing that would have made it worse was if he had looked down at my name written in the palm of his hand when he had said it.

I stole a glance to Ann, who was sitting next to me. She was trembling now. She looked back at me quietly, but she was obviously holding back a million questions. I could almost hear them flying up from her chest and smashing into the back of her clenched teeth one at a time.

"Are you willing to hear what your family has to say to you, Kiffer?" Doug continued from across the table.

There it was again—my name.

Say my name again, and I'll show you what I'm willing to do . . . Doug, I thought to myself. Hearing him say my name made me feel like a child. It scared me to think I had been the topic of discussion without me knowing anything about it, like I had been the topic of an emergency parent-teacher conference to figure out what to do with their problem child.

I swallowed my anger and embarrassment. "Absolutely" was what I said in response, looking around the room at everyone. But I said it in such a way as to convey a surprise that they were concerned at all. I might of well have said, "Oh my god, you are concerned? Please tell me what it is. I'm shocked."

I guess I had decided that my first line of defense in response to whatever they were going to say was to appear surprised. I guess I thought if I could be surprised by whatever they were going to bring up, it would minimize it. But I knew what they were going to say, and I was pissed.

They were about to break the cardinal rule of our family: "If you don't talk about it, it didn't happen." I was confused and angry at them before they ever opened their mouths. Not only were they breaking the rule, but they were also bringing an outsider in. Damn them. What were they doing? As a family, we had been doing the same dysfunctional dance to the same song on the same warped scratched record for as long as I can remember, and now they were about to change the tune. *Screw you*, I thought to myself. *You people wanna do battle in public? Fine. You wanna drag all my shit out of the closet and into light of day? Let's do it! But I'm gonna make damn sure that you are the ones that leave this room in a straitjacket. Bring it on!"*

"They have prepared some letters," Doug continued. "Wyatt, why don't you start." He looked to his left and nodded at my brother. "And then we can go around the room, OK?"

The paper trembled slightly in Wyatt's hands as he started to read the letter he had prepared. He told the story about a time he had been with me at the pharmacy when I had tried to fill a bad narcotics script. I remembered the story well. As I listened to him tell it, my anger began to fade, and in its place was shame. I had taken him to the pharmacy with me when he was just a kid. Too young to leave in the car, I had to take him in with me. I had been trying to get a prescription filled for pills, and the pharmacist was suspicious and refused to fill it, so I just left. I didn't even know at the time that Wyatt had known there was something wrong with that. I didn't know that he even remembered it. But now I knew. He talked about how it made him feel, and it crushed me. He ended the letter by saying, "You are always the person I looked up to, and I didn't know why you were doing something wrong. I was scared. I didn't want to tell anybody about it. I love you."

After he finished, he laid the paper down on the table, and tears were streaming down his cheeks. He didn't look up from the paper again and never looked at me during the rest of the intervention, and I'm really glad he didn't. Looking him in the eyes may have torn a hole in my soul that time couldn't repair. I loved him so much in that moment and hated myself even more.

All the anger at my family that I had been trying to muster up as a defense mechanism faded.

Doug was right to have lead off the intervention with Wyatt, because he was blameless. I couldn't hide behind simply calling him crazy and misguided like I had planned to do with the rest of the people who would read letters that day. It would have been easy to stand up and scream, "Doug, don't you realize the people who hired you are crazier than me? These are the people who taught me to be as crazy as I am today! Don't you see? These people are crazier than me!"

That's what I wanted to say. But after Wyatt spoke, I couldn't. To be honest, I didn't even hear anyone else's letter. I didn't need to. Wyatt had made the point better than any of the others ever could because his was the unencumbered, raw, honest observation of innocence, and it was dead on the money.

One by one, as everyone finished reading their letter and Ann listened, she became more and more disturbed by what she was hearing. Despite a few erroneous details, everything they were saying was true: false prescriptions, stealing pills, drunken rants at parties, all true. And she didn't know a bit of it, until right then. She was losing her mind.

When they were finished reading, I looked over at her, and she was hyperventilating and wide-eyed.

"Honey, it's OK," I leaned over and whispered.

"Kiffer, what are they going to do?" She started rapid firing whispered questions in my ear. "Are they going to call your residency program? Who are they going to tell? You could get into a lot of trouble!"

Ann had some good points. I silently wondered to myself, *What are they going to do? What lengths are they willing to go to?*

"Kiffer, your family really wants you to go into treatment," Doug said. "I am willing to take you there now if you are willing to go—"

"You can't take him!" Ann blurted. It was the first time she had spoken since the whole ordeal began, looking around at everyone else seated at the table and shaking her head. "No. He's not going with you. I'll get him help." She turned and looked directly at me. "Kiffer, they can't take you . . . Don't let them take you!"

"Honey." I put my arm around her shoulders, leaned in, and whispered in her ear, "Let me handle this."

Saying I would handle anything at this point was a ridiculous statement to make, especially considering I hadn't handled anything about my narcotic addiction for years. But I still didn't know what my family was capable of doing at that point. What length were they willing to go to in order get me to treatment? Would they talk to my residency director? Would they talk to the hospital? The police?

The point was, no matter how right they were, I didn't know whom I could trust to help me. I had spent years building a career that could come crashing to the ground if I was found out to be a narcotic addict who had broken the law countless times to get drugs.

I looked around at the faces of my family. They were all looking at me now, silently begging me to agree to go to treatment. They looked hopeful that I would agree to go, but were they willing to put up a fight if I didn't? I knew I couldn't take that chance.

"Yes," I said finally. "I'll go to treatment."

Everyone in the room breathed a long sigh of relief. Everyone except Ann, that is. She was terrified.

"Kiffer, don't go with them. You don't have to—" she pleaded, but I stopped her again.

"Ann, it's going to be OK. I will straighten this out."

Although my family was right, that I was a drug addict and needed treatment, Ann wasn't sure of this. After all, on the outside, the functional addict was the only person she had ever known. I had been using when I met her and using when we got married. So to her, my family's actions looked insane. They had not included her on the plans to perform an intervention on her husband. They decided it best to not include her. She had witnessed my family do some crazy things in the past, but this stunt had to look like the craziest cake topper of them all. And now they wanted to take her husband away and lock him in a mental institution. So needless to say, she was not on board.

Ann just sat, shook, and sobbed.

My mother mouthed the words "Thank you" from across the table.

"Fuck you" was what I wanted to mouth back to her. But I didn't. I just smiled.

For those of you who think that sounds heartless to say in the face of one of the most painful and compassionate things a mother can do for her child, you are right. It was heartless. But from my vantage point, my mother was taking more narcotics everyday than I was. She just had a doctor prescribing them. And that doesn't make it OK. I was just jealous. Why do you get to use pills and I get to go to treatment? I felt like I was being punished for being exactly what the rest of my family had taught me to be.

I was wrong, of course. I would later (much later) realize that my family was doing the only thing they knew to do for me. They were doing something for me that I could not do for myself. I am eternally grateful.

Not long after the intervention, my grandmother Eunice died, and she never got the chance to see me get sober. I think she knows. In fact, I think she's helping me tell you this story—my story, her story, our story. Thank you, Grammy.

I'd like to tell you that after the intervention, Doug carried me off to treatment and I lived a happy, sober life after that. That's not what happened.

Six hours after I checked myself in, I checked myself out. I went back to work like nothing had happened.

I didn't speak to any member of my family involved in the intervention nor did I breathe a sober breath for three more years.

Until two agents from the medical board stepped into my office.

III

SOBERING UP

No Strings Attached

When the agents had left my office that day, they left only one thing: a court order.

When they showed up, I had been sure I would leave with them handcuffed and degraded, being escorted out of the building in front of my patients and staff, head down and humiliated. That was not what happened at all.

After I told to them the story of my life, all the gruesome details of my past behaviors, I found out they already knew most of what I had told them. As a result of an ongoing investigation, they had gathered all the necessary pieces of my story before ever showing up at my office. I'd not known it at the time, but any amount of bullshit I could have fed them would have been carefully discredited with evidence they already had in their possession.

So I suppose after listening to my tearful admission and having pity on my soul, they presented me with an option: I could be charged with all the fraudulent prescriptions I had written over the years, which numbered in the thousands, or I could go to drug treatment.

I signed a court order stating I would do just that and not practice medicine until my treatment was completed. And then they left. Just like that, they were gone.

As I sat in the intake waiting room of the treatment facility a week later, I stared down at the court order I had signed. It looked very official—with the state seal at the top, a raised notary stamp, and a judge's signature just above the one I myself had signed. I just stared down at the paper.

The furniture in the large waiting room was of the sterile variety. Green vinyl upholstery stretched over industrial foam between wooden frames made up the many long benches. No doubt it had to be industrial grade considering the amount of diarrhea and vomit that withdrawing alcoholics and addicts had a tendency to spontaneously spew from their bodies. I should know.

But I was OK. I was in no danger of withdrawing. In my suitcase was a bottle of over a hundred methadone. During the few hours that I waited to be checked into the rehab, I would nonchalantly reach in the side pocket of the suitcase and chew up one of the methadone. I did so right in front of the intake staff behind the large wooden lacquered reception desk. *What did I have to lose at this point?* I thought, chewing up the chalky pills one after another.

And so I sat, staring at walls covered by what was assuredly the twentieth or thirtieth coat of bile-resistant paint and chewed-up pills.

I looked down frequently at the cell phone in my lap when the screen would blink to life, heralding an incoming call. Although I had silenced the phone days earlier, it would still quietly alert me when calls came through.

"You have 119 unread messages."

I guess people were worried.

I had, after all, just left my life. Gone. No farewell. No explanation. Just gone. And people wanted to know why. Some of them, I am sure, had genuine concerns, but most were gossipmongers who only felt better about their life when they could hear about how somebody else had fucked up theirs. So I wouldn't give them the satisfaction.

One day here, next day gone. I had retreated into a self-induced solitude. Too embarrassed to tell more than a select number of people what had happened to me, I hid even from my own phone, a cellular iron curtain.

It blinked to life again.

"You have 120 unread messages."

Looking down at the phone, I dreaded whatever disasters were brewing in my absence. I had left for treatment not being able to tell even those people exactly how long I would be gone or whether I would even be able to return to being a doctor once I got back.

The truth was, over the years I had built a fully fictional but functional mannequin of myself that I presented to everyone I knew. This likeness was a capable, hardworking doctor that could be relied upon to do anything you ask him to do. He was consistent and steadfast. His disappearance was out of character. Now, the shell of myself had broken, and I did not want anyone to see the scared, soft underbelly of a man that was underneath.

The phone blinked to life again.

"You have 121 unread . . ."

"Oh, for fuck's sake!" I said as I threw the phone back into the duffel bag at my feet.

The alarmed face of the receptionist popped up from behind the reception desk as she stopped midsentence in her phone conversation and looked in my direction.

Embarrassed, I imagined the fingers of the hand not holding the phone to her ear were inches away from some panic button underneath her desk. I envisioned, if the button were to be depressed, a team of drug-treatment security exploding from a hidden door in the aged Sheetrock to tackle me and inject a massive dose of Haldol into my roughly exposed ass cheek.

Scared and embarrassed, I held up both hands above my head and mouthed the words "I'm sorry."

Furrowing her brow and placing her free hand over the mouthpiece of the phone, she mouthed back "It's OK."

She stared at me for a few more seconds and then, irritated, took the phone away from her ear and said, out loud this time, "You can put your hands down now, Mr. Cole."

I looked up at both my hands and realized they were still suspended above my head. I snatched them down and back into my lap and forced a self-conscious "see, I'm not crazy" laugh, which succeeded only in sounding a whole lot crazy.

After a forced and irritated smile, she went back to her conversation.

Jesus, maybe I am crazy!

The thought came out of nowhere.

I have lived an entire thirty-two-year life to get to here. I consciously looked around the empty waiting room. *A mental hospital.*

I sighed and reached for another pill out of my duffel bag.

"Kiffer Cole?" a voice called out and stopped me from retrieving the pill.

I looked up and saw a male nurse in scrubs holding a file that presumably held all my pertinent information. I hadn't seen him approaching while I had been digging in my bag for a pill and was startled to hear him say my name.

"Yes," I answered, "that's me."

"Are you ready to go?"

"Yes," I answered, scurrying to my feet and gathering up my duffel bag and suitcase.

"Well, let's go then," he said with a way too chipper tone and practiced smile. I instantly hated him. But I got up anyway and followed him down a long gray corridor leading from the intake waiting room to the detox ward, wheeling my suitcase behind me and duffel bag thrown over my shoulder.

"How are you?" he asked over his shoulder as we strode down the long, slanting walkway.

"Fine," I automatically lied in response.

If I had been even remotely honest, which I was absolutely incapable of being at this point in my life, I would have seethed through gritted teeth, "How am I? How the fuck do you think I am? My life just stopped like a steaming stalled car on the side of the goddamn interstate, and all I can do is stare down into a spewing, spitting, broke-ass engine and scratch my head. I'm going to rehab, yay! How's your dumb-ass day going, retard?"

"Thanks for asking," I added instead.

Thankfully he didn't continue his pointless conversation, maybe because he sensed the extreme unintentional sarcasm in my response, and we continued walking in silence.

When we finally entered the atrium of the detox ward, I was surprised at the size. It was roughly the size of a Little League baseball field, with fifteen-foot ceilings and reinforced glass windows lining the walls from top to bottom, allowing sunlight to flood the massive room.

Dozens of people milled about the ward. Orderlies and patients were moving in random trajectories throughout, and it was easy to tell them apart not only because the staff wore scrubs or nametags but also because they moved faster and with more purpose than the patients did. The patients, who outnumbered the staff ten to one, shuffled rather than walked. The heavy antipsychotic detox medications coursing through their bloodstream slowed their movements down to about half the speed of a normal human cadence. I noticed also that even the patients who were not so heavily sedated padded awkwardly across the floor because their shoes had no shoestrings. I incorrectly surmised that the laces had been removed lest the person needed to be subdued and it wouldn't take much effort on the part of the orderlies to do so. I was later corrected and told that we couldn't have shoestrings because we might decide at some point to hang ourselves or strangle another patient, and this was one less apparatus available to accomplish that task.

The room was bloated with mental illness.

To my left, a woman was on a phone attached to the wall, screaming at someone on the other end, and I could easily hear her end of the conversation.

"Momma, I don't give a fuck what the doctor said, I ain't no drug addict . . ."

Her free hand was holding an unlit cigarette and accentuating wildly every word she was saying to Momma as if she were conducting a concerto of vulgarity.

Standing next to her was an unshaven man saying nothing but only pretending to talk on an imaginary phone held to his ear. Although saying nothing, he was matching the woman's body language precisely, flailing his arm in the air and even pretending to hold and unlit cigarette as she did. She hardly seemed to notice him mocking her as she continued screaming at Momma.

"I didn't steal your goddamn pills, Momma!"

Listening to the conversation, I felt sorry for Momma. I knew from my own personal experience as a narcotic thief that her daughter really had stolen her mother's pills and would probably do it again. I imagined that Momma would rather have been talking to the mute, unshaven schizophrenic than listen to another second of her daughter's load of bullshit.

"Kiffer," my escort called out to me from across the room. I hadn't realized I had stopped in my tracks to take in the scene.

"Come on over here to the nurses' station," he said and beckoned with a wave of his hand.

I started to walk toward him and almost collided with a large black orderly.

"Excuse me," I said, surprised and backing out of his path.

"No problem," he said, stepping around me and continuing on his way. I watched as he passed and noted that he was following one of the other patients closely, matching him almost step for step, stalking him around the room, and never letting him get too far ahead like a predator stalks its prey, and wondered what all that was about.

"Kiffer," I heard again from across the room.

"I'm coming," I said and started toward the nurses' station again.

I wound my way through the sea of psychotics, with my duffel bag and suitcase in tow, and met up again with my guide.

"The nurses will take care of you now," he said, handing my chart over the desk to one of the women behind the chest-high wooden partition that separated the nurses' area from the general population. "Have a good day," he punctuated our brief encounter and giving one last stupid-ass smile before he walked away.

When he was gone, the nurse that had taken my chart from him asked, "Are you Kiffer Cole?"

Her accent was thick Jamaican, and her name tag simply read Carla, RN. No last name. She was short and had reading glasses perched on the end of a short bulbous nose.

"Um, yes . . ." I said, stuttering as if I was unsure. I was irritated she got to use my whole name and all I knew of her was her first name, Carla.

"I think . . ." I said dramatically, pausing long enough to make sure she could see me squint mockingly at her name tag, "Carla . . . that I might be in the wrong place?"

"Are you Kiffer Cole?" she asked again, this time punctuating her question by placing a hand on her hip and looking down and over her reading glasses.

"Well, yes—"

She abruptly interrupted, "Then you are in the right place, baby."

Setting my chart down and walking to the end of the desk, she opened a waist-high swinging door and continued, "Now slide your bags through the door."

"No, really," I said, hurrying to follow her to the end of the desk. My duffel bag fell off my shoulder, forcing me to drag it with my elbow across the linoleum floor as I tried to catch up with her.

"I'm not crazy," I continued, finally catching up with her. "Not like," I paused and motioned with a head tilt over my shoulder toward the general patient populace behind me, "these people." I consciously said *these people* with a whisper, never breaking eye contact with Carla. I needed her to seriously understand that I was different.

Still holding the swinging door open, and after a long irritated pause, Carla leaned closer to me and, matching the same volume level as my whisper, said, "These people," she mimicked my head tilt toward the other patients, "are going to save your life one day."

Her response shocked me. I stared for a long time at her, trying to comprehend what she had said, and it simply wasn't registering.

"What do you mean save my life? I don't know these people."

"Oh, you don't?"

"No, and I don't plan on knowing them after I leave here either!" I could feel my face flushing with blood and anger tightening my throat.

"Baby, you know everything there is to know about these people."

"What?" Her accent was beginning to infuriate me.

"You just don't know you know. And that's why you are here." She glanced around the room and back at me again. "To figure out what you have in common with all these folks."

"What? What do I have in common with them?" Right before she answered, I saw something in her eyes: a recognition, a remembering of something that maybe even she had forgotten up to that moment. Her stern exterior gave way to that memory, and embracing it, she smiled just a little.

"You have to find your soul again."

Uncontrollable tears began to stream down my cheeks.

As if her words had pulled back the heavy, dust-laden drapes in a long-neglected room of my heart, I was now left without the protection of darkness.

"You see," she said, "all these people are hurting like you have been hurting, baby, not because you did anything wrong, but because you didn't know how to do anything right."

I listened as tears continued to fall.

"Everybody here is here because there was nowhere else for them to go. You're just like that, aren't you? The only thing bigger than love in you is the hatred you've got for yourself. Why don't you try to give that up? Give it up just for today, and do what we tell you. Tomorrow, if you wanna go on doing things your way and hatin' on yourself . . . well, I guess you could do that. But why don't we wait and see."

She glanced down at my bags again.

"You wanna slide those bags my way? Or do you want me to call and have somebody take you back out the way you came?"

I glanced down at my bags and knew she was damn sure right about one thing: I really did have nowhere else to go.

I kicked my bags across the threshold of the nurses' station and through the swinging door Carla had been patiently holding open for me. The last of the pills I had in my possession were in that bag, and I knew I'd never see them again.

I looked up, and through my tears, I could see Carla was smiling.

"Good, baby."

She shot a glance down at my feet.

"Now, how 'bout unlacing those shoes."

Hooked on a Feeling

After Carla took my shoestrings, I was forced to stand and watch her and another nurse go through my bags. I stood like a statue and peered over the high nurses' station as they went through everything, shaking out clothes, emptying pockets, and confiscating my shaving kit. I felt like I was at the airport.

But then it got bad.

They pulled out my bottle of methadone.

It was a big bottle too, a tall big-barreled bottle that rattled heavily when she removed it from the bag and inspected the label. Ironically, it was the only bottle that I had ever legitimately gotten from a doctor, so it actually had my name on the label. When the agents from the medical board had come in my office and relieved me of my prescribing privileges, I had actually manipulated another doctor in the community into giving me the prescription. I had never been brave enough when I was forging prescriptions to write for many more than 30 or 40 pills at a time because I didn't want to raise any suspicions at the pharmacy. But my new "legitimate" prescription had over 120 pills in the bottle, and it sounded beautiful to me when it shook—heavy and safe.

But now it was in Carla's hand, and I was panicked. I felt like she was holding a piece of my intestines, like I was watching it grotesquely trailing from a gaping gut wound in my stomach, out and over the desk into her hands as she inspected it closely. Those pills were as much a part of me as any organ in my body, and maybe more important. My adult life had become entirely about the getting and using narcotics to function, and it was out in the open now—my shame, my secret.

She set the bottle down on the desk amid the other confiscated belongings. She then put the other things I was allowed to have back in my bags and slid them back to me through the low swinging door.

"Tim and Ron will take you to your room now," Carla said as she motioned for two of the orderlies to come over from across the room.

When they arrived, the shorter, skinnier of the two stuck out his hand to shake mine.

"My name is Tim," he said. He had a surgically repaired large cleft lip and palate, so when he said his name, it sounded like he said, "My name is Phlegm."

During my entire stay in rehab, I would have to consciously refrain from calling him *Phlegm* whenever I saw him, because that was all I heard in my head from that point forward.

Ron was a taller and heavier-built man. They both accompanied me to my room, which I thought was odd. But it all made sense when we arrived and they closed the door behind us. I put my bags on one of the unoccupied twin beds and was shocked when I turned to face Tim and Ron again.

Tim was stretching latex gloves over his small hands.

Ron was standing next to him with his arms folded over his bulky chest.

"Sir, can you remove your clothing and hand it to me," Ron said in a deep voice. "Tim is going to do your body search while I inspect your clothes."

So there it is then, I thought to myself. *First they take my methadone, and here is where they remove my dignity.* As I took off each article of clothing and handed it to Ron, I noticed the size of his hands. They were as big as the rest of his body. Knowing what Tim was about to do to me, I was grateful it wasn't Ron who was wearing the latex gloves.

After I had undressed, Tim inspected me—*all* of me. Every fold, nook, and cranny of my body was manually scrutinized.

"OK," said Tim as he snapped off the gloves, "go ahead and get dressed. When you're done, come on out, and we will take you to group."

Grope? Isn't that what you just did to me? I thought. But I realized immediately I had misheard him and registered what he was saying.

"Oh . . . OK," I said, starting to put my underwear back on. "Can I go to the bathroom first?" Maybe it was something about having another guy fondle my testicles that made me want to pee, or maybe I just needed some alone time after being manhandled.

"Sure," Ron broke in. "We need a urine sample anyway. I'll go get a cup"

After Ron had returned with the cup and I had had some uncomfortable pillow-talk alone time with Tim, I retreated into the bathroom. I was thankful they let me go alone. After all, they knew without a doubt at this short point in our relationship I wasn't carrying any fake pee on me.

As I stood over the toilet, dangling the head of my penis above the ridiculously small opening of a specimen cup Ron had given me, I realized something: no matter how bad you have to go, when someone says you *have* to go, you seemingly can't go. I stood there looking down at the cup confused. *I had to go a second ago*, I thought. But now I can't go.

My attention wondered.

I looked around the bathroom and noticed it had some peculiarities. The shower was of the walk-in variety but had no shower curtain and no shower rod. The towel hooks were strange too. Three short metal nubs jutted directly up and out of the tiled wall at head height. I walked over and touched one of them. It seemed normal enough until I applied a small amount of pressure downward and the hook gave way and pointed downward. When I removed my hand and thus the pressure, the hook sprang back up like a tiny metal erection.

Oh my god, I thought as I figured it out. *I am in a place that has to have special breakaway towel hooks so we don't hang ourselves!*

I started imagining a scene where some desperate patient (who might have even had this room), depressed and crazed from years of drug use and withdrawals, chewing through their bedsheets and tearing them into strips to make a noose. Finally deciding to end all their misery and pain once and for all, they cinch the noose around their neck and hang the other end over the towel hook. Taking what they think will be their last breath and with the last ounce of emotional energy they have, they leap and pull their knees to their chest—"Good-bye, cruel world"—only to have their ass hit the floor when the fucking trick towel hook breaks away.

How disgraceful would that be? Compounded by the fact that they would have to schlep back to Carla, the Jamaican Jerk, RN, tattered sheet in hand and ask for another one since I presumed it does get cold at night . . .

There was a knock at the door.

"You OK in there?" I recognized the nasal monotone as Tim's.

"Yeah," I answered, not realizing I had been lost in suicidal ideations and forgotten that I had to pee.

I squeezed out half a cup and, upon exiting the bathroom, handed it back over to Tim, who put on his latex gloves again to handle my piss. I think maybe he enjoyed wearing them too since he seemed to have an endless supply in his pockets. Either that or I wasn't the first or last ass he had searched that day.

Tim and Ron then led me back through the large main room and then through a series of locked security doors. We finally arrived at the group therapy room, and I could see it was already underway. Chairs were arranged in a circle, and about half were already occupied, and Tim motioned for me to take one of the empty chairs.

"Kiffer is new," Tim said before exiting the room and leaving me there.

"Welcome," said a man seated on the far side of the circle and holding a clipboard. "I'm Champ. Welcome to the group."

As I sat down, I noticed Champ was older than most of the group, with graying hair and thick black glasses that looked out of place. They looked the kind of safety glasses that athletes wore during games.

"I was just going over the rules of the group, and since you are new, I will repeat them. There will be no physical violence or cross talk when someone is speaking. When it's your turn, you identify yourself and check in with a feeling word and if you need time in the group."

I was already confused.

"And since you are new," Champ said directly to me, "would you like to start?"

No, I thought. All the eyes in the group turned in my direction. But I decided to wing it instead.

"My name is Kiffer." I paused, trying to remember the instructions. "And I feel fine."

When I said *fine*, some of the other members of the group snickered.

"Quiet down," Champ interrupted the laughter. "We don't use the word *fine* here, Kiffer. We try to use words that describe how we are really feeling inside. *Fine* is a cop-out word that rarely describes how we are really feeling inside."

Well, I guess you could have made that one of the rules, Champ, I thought but didn't say.

"What does *fine* usually mean, group?" Champ asked.

In unison, the majority of the people chimed, "Fucked-up, insecure, neurotic, and emotional."

"Right," Champ said, obviously pleased with how his training of the group was going so far. "Why don't we start with someone else, Kiffer, and you can get the flow of the group from listening." He looked down at the clipboard searching for a name. "Jim!" He looked up to the man sitting on my right. "We haven't heard from you today."

The man sitting next to me sat up a little straighter. He looked to be in his early thirties, about the same age as me, and was wearing a T-shirt and blue surgical scrub bottoms. I wondered if he was a doctor too.

There was a long pause as he stared at Champ, obviously annoyed at having been called on.

"My name is Jim, and I'm an addict," he finally said, sounding much more practiced at addressing the group.

"Hi, Jim," the group responded.

"And I'm feeling . . ." Jim continued, "fuck you."

Some of the members started laughing. But strangely, so did Champ. I was confused. Why hadn't that pissed him off?

"I understand," Champ said, continuing to laugh. "Now that was an honest response. But why don't we go with *angry* as your feeling word for now, OK, Jim?"

"You're in charge," Jim said smiling, and he even seemed to lighten up a little.

I took a closer look at Jim now and noticed his fingernails were manicured. When he smiled, his teeth were perfect, white and straight, suggesting thousands of dollars' worth of work. When he spoke, it was direct and with confidence, and his mannerisms made me guess he was gay. Not flamboyant or over the top, but just refined enough to not be your run-of-the-mill straight guy.

As the laughter died down, Champ said, "Why don't you tell the group what brought you here, Jim?"

Without missing a beat, Jim said, "A stretcher and an ambulance."

The room again erupted into even more laughter. Jim became my favorite person in treatment from that moment forward.

"No, really, Jim, why did you come here?" Champ continued to probe further.

"No, really," Jim continued to meet Champ's questioning cadence word for word. "I came because I died."

I realized then Jim wasn't just being intentionally sarcastic for entertainment value. He was actually telling the truth. It just happened to be entertaining.

Jim settled back in his chair a bit and let out a deep breath as if he was resigned to start telling the truth, and he was.

"I came here because I killed myself."

With that statement, the room became death knell silent. Jim had everyone's undivided attention. It was if everyone in the room recognized someone was about to say some real shit and they needed to listen.

Even Jim's toothy white smile disappeared and was replaced by a fixed jaw and slightly tremulous lips when he spoke.

"I killed myself in my office," Jim continued as he stared down at the floor in front of him, eyes unfocused, and remembering. "I injected anesthetics in my office all the time. I'm a dentist and do surgical procedures. Since I'm licensed to administer IV narcotics, I always had leftover drugs, or made sure I did anyway. After I was done with patients, I would take the leftovers into the bathroom and inject myself. But this time, I gave myself too much. I wasn't trying to kill myself . . ."

Jim paused, as if trying to remember something that was just out of reach then continued, "Anyway, when the girls in the office couldn't find me after a long time and the bathroom door was locked, I guess they figured I was in there, and they broke the door down. When they found me, they said I wasn't breathing and I was blue. When the paramedics got to me, I didn't have a pulse, and they started doing CPR. By the time they got me to the hospital, they had brought me back."

Jim paused again to look up at me and then around at the other members of the group. I wanted him to keep talking, to keep telling the story. My mouth was dry, and my palms had started sweating. I had never heard anyone else tell a story like this one. Not that I hadn't heard my fair share of terrible stories, but this was different, very different. Here was someone like me, a doctor, a drug addict, telling people he didn't know the most painful thing he had ever been through, and despite the differences in the details, he was telling my story. I had done drugs in my office. I had stolen drugs from patients. I felt connected to him and his pain. I didn't feel alone. As I watched the tears begin to stream down his face, I understood instantly what nurse Carla had told me when she had said, "Baby, you know everything there is to know about these people." She had been right. My brain didn't know anything about them, but my heart did—my pain did.

"And so after a long time in the hospital," Jim continued, "they transferred me here. I've been here for two days, and I don't know what the hell I'm going to do. I don't know what's going to happen to me. I don't know if I will ever be a dentist again. I just don't know anything."

Applause from the rest of the group erupted after Jim finished, and he looked just as shocked as I was at their response. People were smiling and nodding their heads in approval, in identification. His story was theirs. The details may have been different for everyone, but the feelings were all too familiar. No one was frowning with sadness or judgment. No one was saying, "Oh, I'm so sorry that happened to you. Maybe you can let this be a lesson to you." No, everyone was happy, even proud at what he had said. I began to feel the heat in my own eyes as the tears began to fall, and I realized for the first time I wasn't alone. In fact, I was home.

Slamming on the Brakes

After the group meeting was over and most of the people had had a chance to talk, we were ushered back into the large atrium, where all the other patients were. I wasn't sure where I was to go next, so I went back to find Carla at the nurses' station.

"Do you know where I am supposed to go now?" I asked her.

"Nowhere," she said. "You just hang out until lunch."

"Hang out?" I said. "Shouldn't I get some medication for my detox?"

Carla smiled and laughed a little. "Honey, you aren't in withdrawal yet. The protocol for your treatment says you don't get any medications until you are in full withdrawal."

"Oh," I said as my heart sank at the realization of what she had just said. *Full withdrawal,* I thought. *My god, I haven't been in full withdrawal in years!* I could feel my pulse quicken with fear.

"So just hang out until lunch time, OK?" she said and returned to her paperwork. She might as well have said "Quit bothering me" because I got the message loud and clear.

I wanted to tell her that I had taken a handful of methadone in the intake area and that it would be a couple of days before I was in full withdrawal, but I didn't. I knew that it would take at least forty-eight hours before I was feeling the full effects of methadone withdrawal, and during that time, the drug would begin leaking out of my body. It was going to be hell! Didn't she know that? Didn't she care?

"Carla," I continued. "I just need—"

She stopped me by putting a finger in the air, never looking up from the paperwork she was working on.

"Go talk to Michael." She took the same finger she had just shushed me with and pointed over my shoulder and to the left of the room. "He got here a couple days before you. You guys have a lot in common. He's over there on the couch in the green jacket. Tell him whatever you are about to tell me."

I looked to where she had pointed and saw whom she was talking about. A young man in an olive-green military jacket was sitting slouched on the couch with his head thrown back onto the headrest.

"Carla, that's a patient. I need to—"

The same finger shot into the air again to quiet me.

"What you need to do is do what I tell you," she said, never once looking up again from her work.

Exacerbated, I knew I had worn out my welcome and patience with Carla. I turned and slowly made my over to the man Carla had pointed. I recognized him. When I had arrived that morning, before the group meeting, he had been the one that was being followed by one of the large orderlies, keeping pace behind him and watching his every move. As I got closer to him now, I could see that standing behind him, where he was slouched on the couch, was a different but just as ominous-looking orderly.

"Are you Michael?" I said, stopping in front of him.

"Yeah," he said, obviously startled, sitting bolt upright and opening his eyes. "Is it time for meds?"

"Umm . . . no," I said. "My name is Kiffer. I'm new." I motioned over my shoulder and continued, "Carla told me to come over here and talk to you."

"Oh," he said, breathing out heavily the word in disappointment. "OK."

He scooted over, making a place for me on the couch, and returned to his reclined position, head back and eyes closed.

I took the spot he had vacated. Not knowing what to say or ask, I just sat there and looked around the room. If it hadn't been for the massive orderly standing behind us with his arms folded, I guess to any observer it would have looked like two buddies sitting on the couch with each other watching football.

After sitting there in silence for an uncomfortable amount of time and watching other patients wander around the large atrium, I realized Michael was not going to strike up any sort of conversation with me. I looked over at him. He was wearing Ralph Lauren slacks and slip-on Sperry loafers. He looked like he was in his early thirties like me and, despite the comfortable temperature in the room, was bundled up in an oversized green military jacket that looked like something his father might have brought home from Vietnam. It was tattered and littered with cigarette burns and splotches of other unrecognizable filth from god knows what from god knows where. It was disgusting and didn't at all match up with his stylish pants and shoes.

With his head leaned back on the couch, I would have mistaken him for being asleep if it hadn't been for his legs. Unlike the rest of his body, they were buzzing with constant motion—not pedaling in the air or flying wildly about, but incessantly rubbing against each other. He was like a man-sized cricket attempting to call out to one of the female patients and mate with her. I remembered the woman that had been screaming at Momma on the public phone earlier. I imagined her suddenly stopping midprofanity when she heard Michael's crazy cricket-mating call and saying "Momma, I gotta' call you back!" before hanging up the phone to come find Michael and tear off his designer slacks and shoes.

"I can't make them stop," Michael said without opening his eyes. I had been lost in the daydream and didn't even know he had seen me staring at him.

"When I withdraw, I can't make my legs stop moving,"

His accent was a thick, unmistakable old-money Southern drawl. When he said the word *withdraw*, it sounded like it had three syllables and took twice as long to say. I guessed him to be from Virginia or North Carolina.

His slow, relaxed vocal cadence was contrasted by the frantic movement of his legs.

I knew exactly what he was talking about. I had experienced it many times over the past few years when I ran out of pills. That is to say, back when I still ran out of pills, since I hadn't allowed myself to run out in years for this very reason! I had forgotten that was what was going on with Michael. It all made sense now. I had never seen another person going through what I had gone through.

When it happens to normal people, they call it restless leg syndrome. When it happens to addicts withdrawing from drugs, they don't have a fancy word for it because who gives a damn about addicts anyway, right? The first time it happened to me, I thought I was losing my mind. I was trying to sleep, and my legs felt like the bones had decided they didn't want to be on the inside of the skin anymore. It felt like my shins had decided they were going to vibrate at such a high frequency they could shatter through the overlying muscle and skin and escape. Saying that they were restless would be like calling Ebola a cold.

It was maddening! And it was only the first sign of opiate withdrawal.

"How many times have you withdrawn?" I finally asked Michael.

"I stopped counting."

Michael still didn't look up at me. Still leaning back into the couch with his eyes closed and arms clutching his chest, cocooned in the oversized jacket, he then told me what Carla had meant for him to tell me.

"I was taking a lot of methadone before I came in here," he said. "It's the worst drug to come off of."

I could feel my heart sink at the realization that I was looking at my near future in Michael.

He continued, "They won't give you any boop until you are about to die. If they give it to you too soon, it will make the withdrawal even worse, and you will try to kill yourself. Trust me," he opened one eye into a slit and looked in my direction and continued, "I tried."

I already knew that what he was telling me was the truth. *Boop* was the slang term for buprenorphine, pronounced [boop-ruh-nor-feen], and was one of the newest detox medications on the market. If given too soon, before full withdrawal had set in, it makes the withdrawal worse and psychologically unbearable. But if it is given at the right time, after full withdrawal has set in, it takes the symptoms completely away. In other words, its administration has to be timed perfectly, or disaster ensues.

"That happened to you?" I asked.

"Yeah, last time I was here. Why do you think I have this gorilla escort behind me?" Michael motioned over his shoulder to the orderly standing squarely within earshot of us behind the couch.

"Isn't that right, Ramone?" Michael said a little louder for him to hear.

"Uh-uh," Ramone groaned, relaxed and unfazed by just being racially slandered. "If I remember correctly, last time you were here, you tried to jump through the window like a fool."

"That's right," Michael chuckled. "And now you get to hang out, watch over me and Kiffer here like a big black gargoyle."

Michael's accent made the word sound like [ga-goyle].

"That's right," Ramone said laughing, seemingly unflappable. "I guess we're just lucky white boys can't jump."

"How many times have you been here?" I asked, surprised that this was not Michael's first detox admission.

"This is the second time I've been here, but I've been in rehab six times total."

"Six times!" I said out loud, shocked.

"Yep," Michael said and then repeated slowly in a tone that suggested I had offended him. "Six times."

"I'm sorry—" I started to apologize, but he interrupted me.

"It's OK, don't worry about it," he said as he unfolded his arms from his chest just long enough to give me a slight wave.

"Why so many times?" I asked not as much to find out more of his story but because I was scared to death that I might have to repeat this process more than once.

"I don't know," he answered as he continued to rub his legs furiously back and forth. "I just have a hard time staying sober." He breathed out heavily and shook his head slightly back and forth like he was trying to make sense of it himself. "You know, I have gotten clean so many times. I just can't stay that way. It just like," he paused briefly, like he was trying to find the right words, "like slamming on the brakes."

"Like what?" I was confused.

"Like slamming on the brakes," he repeated. "You know, when you're driving and somebody in front of you stops suddenly and you have to hit the brakes so you don't hit them?"

"Yeah," I said, still not sure where he was going with this.

"Right after you realize what happened, and you are scared shitless, your heart's pounding, and you can taste the adrenaline in your mouth."

"Yeah." I knew the feeling he was talking about.

"Well, imagine if that feeling never goes away. When I get clean, even after a few days or weeks, I still feel like that. I feel like something's not right. I don't feel right. I feel like," he paused again, looking for the words, "like something's wrong with me, or the world, or I don't know . . . everything. I feel like I just want to run. The only thing that takes that away is if I use again. It's like the drugs make me feel normal. Like everybody else I see in the world. As a matter of fact, the first time I can remember ever feeling normal was when I took drugs. Even when I was a kid I didn't feel right. The first time I took a pill, wham! I said to myself, 'Where's this shit been my whole life?' I don't understand it. My wife can take a pill and it just makes her sleepy and she doesn't want to feel like that. If I take a pill, all I want to do is feel like that. I'm just fucked-up, I guess."

"No!" I said a little too loud. "I feel just like that." I was surprised because I had never heard anyone else say how I had felt my whole life.

Michael smiled a little, although it looked difficult for him to do. "So that's why I can't seem to stay sober," he continued. "It feels like I'm always slamming on the brakes."

I sat quietly and let Michael's words sink in. I understood now why Carla didn't want to answer any of my questions and why she wanted me to talk to Michael instead. I worked up a sufficient amount of courage and broke the silence.

"I take methadone too."

The words came out in whisper but loud enough for Michael to hear. My guilt and shame made it feel like I was saying "I'm a pedophile too," but the admission seemed to please him.

"Oh." He opened his eyes and smiled. "Welcome." He leaned over and stuck out his hand to shake mine. When I took his hand, I could feel it was vibrating with tremors and covered with a sheen of cold sweat.

"So tell me your story," he said as he leaned back and resumed his reclined position.

"Um . . . OK," I stammered. I was getting more practiced at telling other people what I had kept hidden for so long, but it still felt like I was taking my clothes off in front of a total stranger. But this time was different. I had a sense that Michael knew how I felt. He would understand everything I had done to get and use drugs. He had probably done the same things I had done. So I told him my whole story.

He never interrupted but just sat back quietly, smiling with his head back and eyes closed. The only evidence that he was listening was the fact that he would laugh and nod his head up and down with every detail of the story I had never known someone would find humorous or relatable. Every once in a while, he would say "Yeah, I did that" or "Yeah, I felt like that."

As the pieces of my story came out of me, met with acceptance and free of judgment, I became more and more comfortable with where I was. I just wish it hadn't been in a mental institution.

"I get it," he said when I was done. "I get it."

I was happy somebody did.

"Michael P." Carla's voice came over the PA system. "Report to the nurses' station for vital signs."

Michael jumped up quick enough to startle me and started to bolt to the nurses' station. Ramone had to hustle around the couch to keep up with him.

He stopped and turned around long enough to say "Wish me luck!"

"Luck?" I answered back confused. "For what?"

"If my vital signs are bad enough, they will give me my boop!" he said, throwing two crossed fingers up in the air.

"Oh," I said, slowly understanding his excitement as he again started to turn toward the nurses' station.

"Hey!" I called out to stop him. "Michael!"

"Yeah?" he turned but continued to move toward the nurses' station, backpedaling.

"What do I do now?" I asked him.

Michael smiled. "You wait," he said, his voice rising as he continued to cross the large Atrium.

"For what?" I asked.

I could see his smile broaden as he continued to backpedal away. "For hell!"

He had to yell those last words before he turned, fingers still crossed and held high above his head, and trotted toward Carla.

Hell: The Manifesto

Hell came.

Three days into my stay on the detox ward, I started to withdraw. Since I had taken a handful of methadone in the intake wing of the hospital before I got admitted, it delayed my withdrawals until then. Before I came in, my doctor had told me over the phone to cut back on my dose and to not take any the day of admission. I wanted to laugh at him when he had told me this. After all, if I had been able to lower my own dose at any time over the last few years, I would have. Didn't he understand that the whole reason I was in this godforsaken mess in the first place was because I had lost any amount of control over my pill taking? I didn't laugh, though. I had just said, "Sure, I can do that," too embarrassed to admit my complete powerlessness. So I had to sit in detox for three days before the withdrawals even started.

The first thing I noticed was restlessness. I couldn't sit still. It became increasingly impossible to sit through the countless self-help groups. I would twist and turn in my chair. It felt like my ass could sense every synthetic fiber in the weaving of the chair and I had to constantly shift my weight back and forth to get comfortable.

I was also freezing. I remembered how Michael had been bundled a filthy army jacket when I first met him, and I understood now. My entire body was slick with cold sweat, and it was impossible to keep warm.

As the withdrawals progressed, it became increasingly difficult to maintain my basic bodily function. If my bladder was even the slightest bit full, I would have to pee. I couldn't tolerate the sensation of pressure. I would pee every chance I got, and only a dribble of urine would come out. My stomach gurgled loudly and cramped, forcing frequent diarrhea episodes in between the ridiculously futile pissing episodes. I spent a lot of time on the toilet expelling tiny squirts of acidic stool, staring up at the breakaway towel hooks that I had noticed after my body cavity search on the first day.

My mind raced too. Instead of having individualized thoughts, they came racing into my mind in multiples. It reminded me of *Star Wars*. When the Millennium Falcon would jump to light speed, individualized stars became linear and raced by the starship's hull. That was how my mind was working—a jumbled mess of unintelligible, anxious thoughts vying for my undivided, bewildered attention.

It was miserable. And it had just started.

You see, you don't have to have *no* drugs in your body to go into withdrawal. You just have to have *less*. This was especially true with methadone. The truth be told, when my withdrawal started, I most likely still had enough concentrations of methadone in my body to kill a horse. But since it was less than what my brain was used to, owing to a tremendous amount of tolerance over the years, my brain was revolting. But I knew, just as Michael had forewarned, things were going to have to get a lot worse before they could give me any medications to help.

I walked around and talked to other people on the ward during these first stages since it was literally all I could do. I asked everybody who would talk to me about why they were there. I asked them about their drugs of choice and how they used. During my rounds, I began to hate the alcoholics. Since I had been there for a few days, I had seen people who came in drunk one day, and after sleeping off the booze, they would wake up shaky the next and immediately be given drugs that made them as happy and comfortable as they had ever been. One drunk actually made the comment to me, "Wow, if I had known quitting drinking was this easy, I would have done it years ago!" I quietly cursed him and headed off to squeeze out two or three drops of piss then cover the toilet in diarrheal spray.

I didn't like the cocaine people any more than the alcoholics. My roommate, who had shown up one day after I did, was a crack addict. After his body cavity search, he laid down in his bed, wrapped a towel around his head to block out the light, and proceeded to sleep for forty-eight hours straight. Every time I would make one of my frequent trips to the bathroom, I would check to make sure he was still breathing and curse him for being able to sit in one place longer than a second, let alone sleep. *Bastard*, I thought. When he finally did wake up, he unwrapped his head, sat up on the side of the bed, and asked, smiling, "Is it time for breakfast?"

"Fuck you" was how I remembered answering him. He wasn't mad. In fact, when he found out that I was there withdrawing from methadone, he apologized to me. He said he had been in detox before and that he wouldn't wish my hell on anybody in the world, except his ex-wife.

If you have ever been through what I am describing, I wish I could crawl through the pages of this book and give you a hug. I would hold on to you and cry like we had just survived a plane crash because I know. At this point in my withdrawal, I would have done anything to get rid of how I was feeling. It wouldn't have been a choice—it would have been a fact. If there would have been booze, I would have drank it. If there would have been pills, I would have taken them. Hell, if I had known someone there who had recently taken pills, I would have let them vomit in my mouth to get rid of how I was feeling.

If you have never experienced addiction and feel like people continue to do drugs because they want to, because they have some sort of choice, then I would also like to crawl through the pages of this book not to give you a hug but to grab you by the nape of the neck and take you on a tour—a tour of broken souls. I know now, having gone through what I did and being an addiction medicine physician working with addicts every day, that the drug-addicted brain represents a true mental illness, a disease. I would like to introduce you to my patients, some of whom come from the most upstanding, healthy homes but end up committing the most horrendous atrocities to alleviate withdrawal.

I'm not just talking about the nearly half of the federal inmates who are in prison for drug-related crimes according to the Bureau of Justice Statistics. I'm talking about the people you may run into every day. I have patients who underwent years of unnecessary surgical procedures in order to continue getting prescriptions for narcotics, being unaware that whatever pain they had at the initiation of the narcotic use had long since faded years before and that the only thing the drugs were good for now was alleviating withdrawal.

That is the insidious nature of narcotics. Over time, through changing brain pathways, they only succeed in producing the very symptoms that only continued use of narcotics will alleviate. Once physiologic dependency on the drug has been established, people *can't* stop using. It's not a choice. The withdrawal drives them to continue using until they chase the drug through the gates of insanity and death. They are frequenters of emergency rooms, pain management clinics, and surgical suites. To be sure, they all have very real symptoms that are seemingly alleviated only with the use of more narcotics. So to the addict, it appears less like a drug problem than it is a supply problem. When they have drugs, no problem!

I once had a patient so heavily addicted to pain medications that the local emergency rooms forbade her from stepping foot on the premises of the hospital unless she came by ambulance because she had been there so often asking for pain medications. When she continued to show up by ambulance after that, the paramedics in her community actually began refusing to take her to the hospital when they came to her home because she called them so much. She told me during her first visit to my office, "Dr. Cole, those paramedics told me the only reason that they would take me to the hospital is if I had a gunshot wound or someone had stabbed me. Can you believe that? But, Dr. Cole, I was hurting so bad I didn't know what to do, so after they left, I called 911 again and told them to get back to my house because I had a gunshot wound! When I hung up, I loaded my husband's hunting rifle and shot myself in the foot!"

Sitting on that toilet in my third day of detox, I would have gladly shot myself in the foot to get rid of the withdrawals! I remembered Ramone's comment to Michael on my first day at rehab, "You tried to jump through a window like a fool!" I silently wondered if they were going to have to get Ramone to come watch over me as I looked up longingly at the breakaway towel hooks. I'm not saying I wanted to die, but a little asphyxiated unconsciousness was sounding better and better. I wondered if I could get my chipper-ass, crackhead roommate to choke me out a little and, when I came to, choke me out again!

Owing to my extreme cravings, I also began to understand the body cavity search I had endured on my first day. If I had truly understood what was coming, I would surely have tried to stash some pills in any body cavity I could have reasonably (or unreasonably) shoved them inside. While I was on the detox ward, I met a woman who had been caught trying to smuggle in pills in her vagina by hiding them in an empty tampon tube. Before that day, I had never wished I'd had a vagina. When she had told me about how the orderlies had found the pills, I remembered the stripper from years earlier in the ER. I had removed not one but four old tampons. If I had a vagina, I could have surely smuggled in enough pills to carry me through my entire rehab stay as long as nobody looked.

Vaginas truly are amazing. Not only do they have the capability to suck money out of the pockets of men, but you can also carry things in them.

I once had a pregnant woman smuggle her daughter's urine into my office with her vagina. Needing desperately to pass a drug screen to stay out of jail, she had her four-year-old daughter urinate into a bowel at home. After collecting the urine, she transferred it into a condom, tied it off like a balloon, then shoved the condom into her vagina. Since her urine drug screen was going to have to be witnessed by one of the office staff, it had to appear as if the urine came from her. So when she squatted over the toilet and reached down and around her gargantuan pregnant belly with a carefully sharpened fingernail rupturing the condom, it looked like the urine came straight out of her own bladder. Voila!

She almost got away with it. But suspecting she was up to something, my office staff did a pregnancy test on the urine too. When I walked into the room to see her after the urine test had resulted, I said, "Congratulations, you passed your urine drug screen."

"Of course I did," she had said smugly, sitting back and rubbing her obviously pregnant belly.

"And you're also not pregnant anymore."

The smile disappeared from her face. She knew she had been caught.

I don't tell you that story because it's incredible. I'm telling you that story because it highlights what I have come to realize about the nature of addiction: it is not a choice. I could fill this book and volumes like it describing stories exactly like this one. This patient's behavior is not unique.

Addicts don't continue using drugs because they choose to. They continue using drugs because it is a physical, neurobiological impossibility for them to stop on their own.

Despite knowing that if she continued using drugs, she was going to lose custody of her four-year-old daughter, go to jail, and deliver her second child while incarcerated, only to give it up to foster care as well, that patient continued using drugs. This kind of behavior doesn't represent simple bad decision making. It doesn't mean she made bad choices. It means she could not physically stop doing drugs.

Addiction is a mental illness defined by an inability to stop using drugs despite severe adverse consequences. Trying to make addicts stop using drugs by doling out punishments will never work. Incarcerating addicts only results in addicts using drugs while incarcerated. Without intense treatment and rehabilitation, drug addicts cannot stop using drugs on their own. Society will never succeed in taking drugs away from addicts; the addict has to be taken away from drugs and treated. The war on drugs will never be won. However, the treatment of addiction is both possible and plausible.

Drugs have never been the problem. The problem is the brain they go into.

Researchers in the field of addiction medicine have found that addiction as a disease probably originates in the area of the brain called the mesolimbic reward pathway and most likely results from aberrant dopamine pathways and changing neural structures over time. I won't bore you with any further details now—although I do love talking about it. Suffice it to say, the brain of the addict is just not right. If you are an addict or are unfortunate enough to love a using addict, you probably already suspected this already.

The addicted brain simply does not process mind and/or mood-altering substances like normal people do. In this way, addiction is a lot like diabetes.

If a normal person eats a candy bar, their blood sugar may rise slightly but quickly return to normal in short period of time. However, when a diabetic eats the same candy bar, their blood sugar will rise to dangerous levels and will require medication to bring it down. They may even require hospitalization as their diabetes is severe. Does this mean that the candy bar was the problem? Absolutely not. The problem was the body that it went into. Trying to treat addicts by trying to control drugs in our society is just like trying to treat diabetes by limiting access to candy bars.

In the same way that diabetes is not a sugar problem, addiction is not a drug problem. It is a drug metabolism problem that already existed before the drug went in. And once the drug has affected the brain of someone with the disease of addiction, they cannot stop without a tremendous amount of help.

The war on drugs cannot be won and has, in fact, cost our society too much already—in the form of lost dollars and, more importantly, lost lives. Too many men and women in law enforcement have bravely given their lives waging a battle that has only gotten worse over time despite their efforts. But I do not believe they paid an ultimate price in vain. I believe they have helped pave a way to a healthier future, one in which law enforcement will begin to work hand in hand with the addiction treatment community, and I humbly salute them. I trust, and I have to believe, we are entering this new age. I have dedicated my career to it at this point.

Of course, I didn't feel this way in detox.

As I laid in my small twin bed shaking and sweating, I couldn't think about anything else but wanting my withdrawal to go away. Between trying to figure out how to swallow my own tongue and frequent trips to the bathroom, my mind was a knot of tangled threads of remorse and shame. I had never been this deep into withdrawal before, and I felt scared and alone.

On the morning of my fourth day in detox, Ann had been allowed to visit me. Our first son, Anderson, was three months old, and she had had to leave him at home with her parents since children were not allowed into detox visitation.

Patients who had visitors were escorted from the detox ward to the gymnasium to see their family. Simply walking the small distance was almost unbearable for me. My legs ached and felt like if the bones would simply shatter into a thousand pieces, I might feel better. When I entered the gymnasium, I could see metal folding chairs had been set up in groups of twos and threes and scattered across the surface of the gymnasium floor. Scanning the room, I quickly saw Ann in one of the chairs and an empty one for me beside her. I took a deep breath and consciously tried to make myself look composed for her. I tried to walk like my legs weren't screaming in pain and smile like I wasn't the stark raving lunatic that I actually was. I don't know why I wanted to pretend for her, but it only made sense looking back on it now. I had been pretending our whole marriage—not pretending that I loved her (I did), but pretending I wasn't the drug addict that I was, hiding pills, hiding drinking, hiding myself. I didn't know how to stop doing that.

When I made my way across the room to her, she hugged me. I could feel her shaking slightly, and when I pulled away, I couldn't tell if she was scared, angry, or nervous. I had turned her life upside down, and despite being in the middle of severe narcotic withdrawals and languishing bouts of self-pity, I still cared very much about what I was putting her through and desperately wished I could turn it all around.

"How are you doing?" she asked as we sat in our folding chairs.

"I'm OK," I lied. "How is Anderson?" I could feel tears try to surface at the mention of my son's name and consciously fought them back. Swallowing hard, I could feel my chest tremor with each breath.

"He's OK. He's with my mother at home."

"What has she said about all this?" I was worried about what everybody thought of me. I think I desperately wanted everyone in my life to still respect me as I felt my own self-respect slipping dangerously out of my grip.

"She just wants you to get better, Kiffer. We all do."

Her comment made me feel completely alone. I'm sure it was true, that *they* all did want me to get better. But her comment made me feel even more isolated, like there was a *they* and a *me*—a *they* who were infinitely healthier and a *me* who was terminally broken somehow.

"What are they doing for you here?" she asked, glancing around the large gymnasium, skeptically scanning the other groupings of patients and families scattered around the room.

"Well, I go to a lot of groups and talk about addiction and how I'm supposed to get better." A thought occurred to me that there was something that may make her feel better, and I said, "There are a lot of other doctors here with the same problems I have, even lawyers and dentists." My mind went back to my first day and hearing Jim's story in my first group.

"Oh great," she said sarcastically in a tone that suggested this did not make her feel better in the least. My heart sank. I realized that even though meeting other professionals with drug addiction made me feel less alone, it didn't make her feel less alone. I think I wanted her to think of me as less of a piece of shit if she knew there were other people in my position. As it turns out, though, I was the only one who thought I was a piece of shit; she didn't.

"How are you doing?" I asked. It took every ounce of courage I had to ask her that question because I didn't know if my waning self-esteem was ready for the answer. I blamed myself for everything she was going through.

After staring down at the floor for an agonizingly long moment, tears began to fall down Ann's cheeks, and she answered, "I just don't know, Kiffer. I'm scared. They won't tell me how long you are going to be here. No one will talk to me on the phone when I call, and I don't know what we are going to do." She paused, looking around her chair for her purse, and then wiped her tears with her sleeve instead. "They wouldn't let me bring my purse in here. I had some tissues in it."

I cringed because I didn't know the answers to any of those questions either.

"They keep telling me that they take things one day at a time here," she continued. "What the hell does that even mean, Kiffer? They may take things one day at a time, but the world doesn't. We have bills that need to be paid. They won't tell me when you can go back to work. I can't go back to work right now because we have Anderson. What are we going to do?"

The tears were flowing in streams now, and she was sobbing. I watched her helpless, hating myself even more for having put her through this. I had always had answers before. I had always known what to do, what to say, and now I had nothing. Shame draped itself around me, and it seemed everything that was happening was more evidence that I really was the incredible piece of shit I thought I was. I wanted to hold her and tell her everything was going to be OK, but I couldn't. I wanted to give her relief, but I couldn't even do that for myself. The curtain had been pulled back on the lie of my life, and all I could do was stand helpless and naked and feel every soul crushing emotion that came along with it.

What the fuck can I do? I thought.

And then it came.

Seemingly out of nowhere, something came to mind.

I can stay sober.

Edging and elbowing its way past the crowded self-pity and hopelessness, it pushed its way to the front of my awareness. Crawling over and around a thousand hellish voices was the first sober thought I can ever remember having.

I can stay sober!

Sitting there looking at Ann sobbing into her sleeves, wanting so desperately to take her pain away, I realized the only thing I had the option of doing right now was just that: just stay sober.

It was the only thing left to do right now. In that moment, I was doing everything I could do by not drinking or taking pills. Despite wave after bone-crushing wave of remorse and self-criticism, I realized there was no way around it but through it. And I could stay sober. I *could* stay sober. For almost eight years, I had not lived one solitary moment without some form of narcotic or alcohol coursing through my veins, and I had somehow managed to stay sober for four whole days.

I leaned over and took Ann's hands. I could see from the look on her face she was surprised at how shaky I was, and she gasped a little when she looked into my eyes. I remembered how shocked I had been to shake Michael's hand on my first day when he had been going through full withdrawal, how his eyes had looked like gaping black pits of misery, and I knew she was seeing the same things in mine now.

"Ann, I don't know the answers to any of those things now either, but all I can do is what they tell me to do. It's the only thing left for me to do." Her breathless sobs eased just a little. "I know you had no idea about how bad I had gotten, and I am sorry. I don't know how it got this bad in the first place, but the only thing left for me to do is exactly what they tell me to do."

She shook her head yes, knowing intuitively that there really was nothing else that I could say that wouldn't have been a complete line of bullshit. And since that was what I had been feeding her most of our marriage, she seemed even a tiny bit relieved.

When they announced that visitation was over, we stood up and hugged for a long time.

With her head on my chest, she said, "They wouldn't let me bring you any clothes."

"I know," I said. "It'll be OK."

"No, it won't." She pulled away, looking up at me again, and said, "You stink."

Let's Make This Thing Personal

I did stay in treatment. And I did exactly what I told Ann I would do, which is exactly what the people in the treatment center told me to do.

I stayed in official treatment for six months and remained part of their aftercare program for five years. I have not found it necessary to drink or use drugs in all that time and remain sober today. That is the only thing I can tell you I've done right. I have tried to use all the tools sobriety has given me to the best of my ability and have often still fell short of those chosen ideals at times.

My biggest regret is not having been a good husband to Ann. Four years after getting sober, I had an affair, which ended our marriage, and to this day I can't tell you definitively why I did that. I struggled greatly with whether or not I would tell you that about myself, but there it is. I realized that if I was going to write a book about my life, I would have to be completely transparent or not write the damn thing at all. I was afraid of how you would judge me. I feared that getting to the end of this book, you might have grown to like me just a little, only to throw the book into the trash after I told you I was an adulterer as well. But I eventually reasoned that I would much rather you hate the real me than love the liar.

Of all the mistakes I have ever made, I think that one bothers me the most. My struggle with this part of my life is really what has made me question everything. Before I got sober, I could blame all my mistakes on a drugs or a crazy childhood. But it's the things about me now, after the drugs are gone and the covers have been pulled back on my life, that fascinate and disturb me the most.

I've had to ask myself from the beginning of this book, why are you writing this?

From the very first words until what I'm writing you right now, I have questioned my motivations. I mean, it's not like these stories of my life are all that groundbreaking. Hell, I bet a lot of people reading this have had far more interesting, funny, or tragic things happen to them over the course of a lifetime. What I'm saying is that I know I am not blazing new trails.

I also questioned whether or not it was just some bloated narcissistic endeavor meant to inflate my already out-of-control ego. Although arguably this may be a little true, I don't think it was the primary motivation either.

I think I wrote this book to be honest. I wrote it to honor life in general, a life wrought with shortcomings and mistakes, but a life nonetheless. I wanted to reach through the pages and touch your soul in a way I would have liked someone to have touched mine. If this book finds you in a place in your life where you are not even sure whether it's worth living in the first place, I'm talking to you right now: I have felt that way. I have felt at times that everyone in the world had somehow found a way to be happy and I didn't, like they knew some secret and I was clueless.

You know what the truth is?

Most people are full of shit.

They feel just like you do. Just like us. The same person you think has it all together is right now drowning themselves in booze or sobbing on some therapist's couch. I wish you could see them. They look ridiculous.

It's not life that makes us feel like shit—it's our secrets!

Those things about you that you are hiding from the world because you are too embarrassed or ashamed are the very things that make you beautiful. Most of the selfish, arrogant, and dishonest shit I have ever done in my life was a direct result of trying to convince the world that I wasn't selfish, arrogant, or dishonest. The truth is, I am all those things. You are all those things. If that pisses you off, get over it. I have done the most damage to myself and others when I have tried to hide who I really was from them. Does that make me a bad person? Hell no. It just makes me a person scared you won't love me if you ever got to know me. So I hide, I drink, I lie, and I hope you never pull back the curtain to see the Great Wizard of Oz is a small, scared man pulling levers and blowing smoke straight up your unsuspecting ass.

The longer I live sober, the more I realize humanity at large has lost its mind.

By that I'm not suggesting I am some enlightened being floating above it all on some cloud of self-righteousness. No, I am right in the mix with you. All I'm saying is, the only way I have found to maintain some semblance of peace in my life is to accept who I am, what I've done, and whom I've hurt along the way. In doing so, I can move forward and learn to love a little more, care a little more, and hopefully, leave less emotional damage in my wake.

That's why I wrote this book.

I know I'm going to make a lot more mistakes along the way, but hopefully, it won't be because I was too afraid or ashamed to look at why. I hope I honor a life of imperfection and strive only to be compassionate toward myself and others.

In this way, I learn to love life, the same life I tried to destroy with drugs and alcohol, and live it passionately.

I hope my children read this book one day, after having watched me over their lifetime, and can say, "Yeah . . . that makes sense."

The End

Printed in the United States
By Bookmasters